STEWARDSHIP

STEWARDSHIP

A Parish Handbook

C. Justin Clements

Liguori
LIGUORI, MISSOURI

Published by Liguori Publications
Liguori, Missouri
www.liguori.org

Library of Congress Cataloging-in-Publication Data

Clements, C. Justin, 1938–
Stewardship : a parish handbook / C. Justin Clements. —1st ed.
p. cm.
ISBN 0-7648-0662-9 (pbk.)
1. Stewardship, Christian. 2. Catholic Church—Finance. I. Title.

BV772 .C545 2000
248'.6—dc21 00–030648

Liguori Publications, a nonprofit corporation, is an apostolate of the Redemptorists. To learn more about the Redemptorists, visit *Redemptorists.com.*

Printed in the United States of America
09 08 07 06 05 7 6 5 4 3

Dedication

To my professional stewardship and fund-raising colleagues—the true unsung heroes of the nonprofit world—without whose boundless creativity, endless enthusiasm, unique skills, and faithful devotion to service, thousands of charitable, educational, and religious organizations would be unable to deliver their services and conduct their programs. Thank you, and God bless you, one and all.

Acknowledgments

Kudos and thanks to…

Sister Mary Etta Kiefer, OSB, whose special relationship with the English language keeps my muse under control.

Bob Scheitlin, accountant extraordinare, for his remarkable expertise as an estate-planning specialist, and his reliable guidance as a friend.

Attorney John Chappell and canon lawyer Msgr. Charles Koch, whose legal acumen was an invaluable help in sorting out the legal complexities which impact Catholic stewardship.

Bob Heyer and Jean Marie Hiesberger, my unseen mentors and patrons, who honor me with their validation of my work.

Numerous North American Catholic stewardship pioneers—pastors, dioceses, parishes, the International Catholic Stewardship Council, and the U.S. bishops—whose heroic risk-taking and impassioned leadership are never-ending sources of inspiration and motivation.

Shirley, my beloved life partner, and Johnny V., our pride and joy, who all-too-often must compete with a laptop computer for my time and attention.

Jesus Christ, the Magnificent Steward.

Contents

Preface

This book was written primarily for Catholic parishes that are either poised to begin a stewardship conversion journey, or attempting to promulgate a total stewardship way of life. However, *Stewardship: A Parish Handbook* can be used by *any* Christian individual or organization as a guide for the process of stewardship conversion. Its content is based on nearly twenty-five years of development, fund-raising, and stewardship conversion experience. Its purpose is to help parishes, dioceses, schools, or other organizations assess their stewardship conversion efforts and increase opportunities for grateful members or supporters to return to God a fair portion of God's gifts of time, talent, and treasure.

At the outset, I must confess two distinct biases regarding stewardship:

(1) I am a time-and-talent aficionado. My personal and professional experiences have convinced me that people who truly *own* their parishes, or other charitable organizations, will gladly and generously share their financial resources with them. The most emphatic proof of ownership of a church or charity is displayed when people willingly contribute some of their most precious possessions. And, in today's frenetic world, one of our most precious possessions is our time. In other words, I believe that the success of a stewardship conversion process hinges on the ability of a community to inspire its members to freely share their God-given gifts of time and talent. Their stewardship of treasure will inevitably follow.

(2) I am absolutely certain that the solution to many of the world's ills can be found in the stewardship way of life. If every human being would embrace total stewardship as outlined in sacred Scriptures (a require-

ment for Christ's disciples, by the way), most of humankind's problems would dissipate. Of course, it would be a stretch for some Buddhists, Moslems, and agnostics, for example, to accept Christ's stewardship mandate; but any reasonable person can deduce the logical consequences of the global practice of good stewardship.

Living as a good steward is the fundamental, practical manifestation of Christian discipleship. Unfortunately, the stewardship way of life has traditionally received scant attention in schools of theology and seminary education programs. However, thanks to the pioneering efforts of many U.S. parishes, stewardship is steadily rising to its rightful prominence in the faith life of the United States Catholic Church.

This book will provide a comprehensive reference point from which to grasp the totality of the concept of stewardship and the stewardship conversion process. It's a foundation upon which to expand and build through additional reading, study, conversation and, above all, experience.

Who will find *Stewardship: A Parish Handbook* useful?

- Bishops, pastors, pastoral-life coordinators, directors of religious education, stewardship committees, parish councils and finance committees, and neophyte stewardship and development directors seeking to grasp the stewardship "big picture."
- Seasoned development professionals looking for a total stewardship refresher course, as well as validation of the many good things they do.
- Seminary and Catholic school faculty members and students who need to learn more about total stewardship and the stewardship conversion process.
- Anyone who is simply curious about the sometimes elusive and confusing concept of stewardship.

Most of what you will find in these pages is not original; it was gleaned from the generous sharing of knowledge and experience that is a hallmark of my profession. *Stewardship: A Parish Handbook* is most assuredly a work in progress. It is by no means intended to be the last word on stewardship conversion! Therefore, I welcome any feedback to improve what you find here.

C. JUSTIN CLEMENTS
December 14, 1999

INTRODUCTION

What's It All About?

1. THE PUZZLE PIECES

Stewardship is a word which, when heard or read, immediately triggers a unique cluster of thoughts and feelings within each person. Although the concept of stewardship is most at home within the realm of things spiritual and religious, it's a word increasingly used in secular discourse. Industrialists, environmentalists, agribusiness leaders, public servants, and many others frequently refer to stewardship when describing certain aspects of their various disciplines. This expanded societal awareness of the value of stewardship naturally adds even more facets to an already complicated notion.

For a disciple of Jesus Christ, however, stewardship is no puzzle; it's a simple idea. Stewardship is a way of life predicated upon four interlocking concepts: (a) God, the Source, (b) gratitude, (c) accountability, and (d) return.

A. God, the Source

True believers, agnostics, and full-bore atheists all agree on one thing: we'll never get out of this life alive! It's also abundantly clear that we enter the world with nothing and, with the rare exception of the occasional person who is buried in his favorite antique automobile or festooned with her jewelry, we exit with nothing. Everything we accumulate during our passage through time is only temporarily on loan to us.

Christians believe that God owns everything; God is the Source who generously allows us to use and hold in trust these possessions during our mortal journey, beginning with the gift of life.

B. Gratitude

The normal human response toward someone who freely shares his or her property with us is a feeling of gratitude. To be sure, God doesn't *need* our thanks. However, as human beings, as people of faith, and as disciples of Jesus Christ, we need to *express* our gratefulness for the many gifts and blessings we have received.

C. Accountability

The very term *stewardship* implies responsibility. A steward is one to whom certain possessions and duties have been entrusted. Christ's recurring references to stewardship contain an incontrovertible theme of accountability. Stewards are required to use their masters' property wisely and well. Those who do are praised and rewarded; those who don't are excoriated. The scriptural message of stewardship is clear: God demands our accountability for the gifts we are allowed to use between birth and death.

D. Return

From sacred Scriptures we can draw one additional conclusion about Christian stewardship: Jesus Christ expects some yield on his investment in us. Remember what happened to the steward who buried the talent he had received and simply gave it back to the master upon his return! As Christ's disciples, we have an obligation to use God's gifts and talents responsibly, develop them to their full potential, and return them "with increase."

2. CHRISTIAN STEWARD AND TOTAL-PARISH STEWARDSHIP DEFINED

The U.S. bishops in their 1992 pastoral letter, "Stewardship: A Disciple's Response," presented a lucid and eloquent definition of the Christian steward as "one who receives God's gifts gratefully, cherishes and tends them in a responsible and accountable manner, shares them in justice and love with others, and returns them with increase to the Lord."

During a stewardship retreat in 1993, a group of five parish stewardship committees from the Diocese of Evansville, Indiana, saw the need to develop a vision statement for total parish stewardship against which they could measure the progress of stewardship conversion within their communities. Following the lead of the U.S. bishops, the committees collectively crafted this statement:

Vision Statement for a Total-Stewardship Parish

A Total-Stewardship Parish is ALIVE!
It is a prayerful, welcoming, Eucharist-centered
community with a common vision:
God Is the Source of All.
Its members are committed to furthering the word
and work of Christ by caring for each other
and all of God's creation.
In gratitude, they joyfully give back a portion
of their God-given gifts of Time,
Talent, and Treasure.

Today, as they begin each meeting, stewardship committees throughout the Evansville Diocese review their stewardship conversion efforts by asking: "How close are we to achieving the ideal described in our vision statement?" The ideas, suggestions, and information presented in this book were selected and organized to help parishes and other Christian organizations realize this stewardship vision.

3. STEWARDSHIP AND FUND-RAISING

In recent years, the word *stewardship* has suffered the unfortunate misperception that it's just a euphemism for fund-raising. As one layperson observed: "When my pastor says 'stewardship,' a big bell rings in my head that says: MONEY!" Church leaders who labor to bring Christ's challenging stewardship message to those they serve can attest to how much this skewed perception of stewardship hampers their efforts.

Fred Hofheinz, program officer for Lilly Endowment, captured this issue quite clearly in the Spring 1997 issue of *NCSC Resource*:

> Whenever we tie stewardship to concrete, practical things (like contributing to the diocese's annual appeal or volunteering our time at parish events), we run the risk of losing the connection between genuine Christian stewardship and all aspects of our daily lives. But when we say that stewardship is an attitude of mind and heart,

> a way of life, we open ourselves to the possibility that stewardship will influence everything that we say and do—not just the way we spend our time, talents, and treasure.

When, for example, religious organizations refer to their annual fund drives or capital campaigns as "stewardship appeals," they perpetuate the confusion between Christian stewardship as a lifestyle and certain aspects of stewardship of treasure which may indeed include, but are not limited to, fund-raising activities and strategies.

In the pages that follow, we've attempted to present a practical and balanced treatment of total stewardship based on the equality of time, talent, and treasure. There is, however, a reality regarding the process of stewardship conversion that must be acknowledged at the outset: stewardship of treasure includes fund-raising. In recent years, fund-raising has become an increasingly sophisticated enterprise. It's necessary, therefore, to devote a substantial portion of this book to the stewardship of treasure because of the numerous elements contained within the professional discipline of fund-raising—commonly referred to as "development." However, this larger treatment of stewardship of treasure should not be interpreted as placing greater emphasis on treasure over time and talent.

4. THE STEWARDSHIP SOLUTION

Increasing numbers of U.S. Catholic parishes are opting for the "Stewardship Solution": a quantum leap of faith toward total stewardship. This radical transformation typically begins with a profound, public commitment by parish leaders to a continuous process of communal stewardship conversion. The Stewardship Solution is based on a conviction that a parish belongs to each of its members, and it requires each parishioner's personal commitment to a stewardship way of life.

A parish that has chosen the Stewardship Solution is characterized by a heroic communal prayer life, a superb spirit of welcoming and hospitality, and a burning desire to serve the spiritual and temporal needs of all its members. Tithing and proportional sacrificial giving are the rule, not the exception. Opportunities for sharing time and talent abound. If the parish operates a school, faculty members are paid a just wage, and there is no tuition. Outstanding womb-to-tomb religious education is provided. The parish tithes its own income and shares its resources with those in need outside the parish—even other less fortunate parishes. In the words of the vision statement for a total-stewardship parish presented above, the parish is alive and possesses the ten characteristics of a total-stewardship parish found in Appendix 7.

5. STEWARDSHIP CONVERSION: A PROCESS

In 1992, the U.S. bishops promulgated their pastoral letter on stewardship entitled "Stewardship: A Disciple's Response." By linking the stewardship way of life with discipleship in Jesus Christ, the U.S. bishops effectively reminded all Christians that being a good steward is not an option, it's imperative. Developing a stewardship attitude is both a "journey toward" and a "retreat from." It's a journey toward the challenging ideal of the good steward found throughout the gospels; it's a retreat from the "I-me-my" selfishness that the world promotes as a laudable goal.

Stewardship is much more than the things we do with our time, talent, and treasure; it's an attitude, a mentality, a frame of reference, a way of life. For most Catholic Christians, it requires a change of heart, a process of conversion. Listen to the U.S. bishops, who say in their 1992 pastoral letter: "For one who is Christ's disciple there is no dichotomy, and surely no contradiction, between building the kingdom and serving human purposes as a steward does"; and also "Being a disciple is not just something else to do, alongside many other things suitable for Christians, it is a total way of life and requires continuing conversion."

The process of stewardship conversion takes time, demands effort, entails sacrifice, necessitates education, and requires patience. Yet the rewards for individuals and communities are inevitable and inestimable. God will not be outdone in generosity!

6. KEY TO SUCCESSFUL STEWARDSHIP CONVERSION

A new parishioner in a highly successful stewardship parish recently observed: "Every nook and cranny in my new parish exudes stewardship. The pastor refers to it constantly. My fellow parishioners talk openly about their efforts to be good stewards. The language of stewardship is used in every parish publication. Our school children scramble to find ways to share their time, talents, and treasure. Stewardship is just woven into the fabric of our parish—and everyone seems so happy and proud of it!"

"Woven into the fabric of our parish"—this statement expresses the key to successful parish stewardship conversion. The pastor, the staff members, and every parishioner must be committed to the process of stewardship conversion. Parish leaders and educators should take advantage of every natural opportunity to promote the stewardship way of life, beginning with the children of the parish. The language of stewardship should become second nature. Parishioners should be encouraged to share the stories of their stewardship journeys with one another. Stewardship should be a constant theme, not just a "sometime thing."

PART 1

STEWARDSHIP OF TIME AND TALENT

CHAPTER 1

Focus On Time and Talent

1. LAYING THE GROUNDWORK

The average age of priests in one Midwestern diocese has been increasing by one year annually for the past several years. In 1998, it reached sixty years! Using a combination of historic data and demographic projections, a number-crunching pastor calculated that by 2025 there would be one priest still active in that diocese! This diocese and many others in the United States are currently working through processes often called "Future Parish Staffing," the goal of which is to reorganize diocesan structures and redistribute clergy manpower based on a projected reduction in the number of active priests in the coming years.

In many U.S. locales, the shortage of priests has reached crisis proportions. Why is it necessary to mention this ominous predicament in a book about stewardship? Because it has a direct bearing on the emerging preeminence of the stewardship of time and talent for North American Catholics. Not only are disciples of Jesus Christ obliged to *live* as good stewards, more than ever U.S. Catholic laypersons are being called to assume active, high-profile responsibility for the life and operation of their parishes and dioceses.

Furthermore, any reference to stewardship of time and talent in today's Church must include some commentary about the pace and change in today's world. Societal and technological changes which formerly developed over decades and generations now take place in a matter of weeks or days. Instant communication has turned the planet into a large, polyglot community. Rapid scientific advances create almost daily moral and ethical dilemmas for Church leaders.

The Catholic Church is not immune from this climate of change. Some Catholics still long for the "good old days" when everything about the Church was well-defined, to-the-point, cut-and-dried. Sin was sin. The *Baltimore Catechism* ruled, at least in the United States. Everything had its place, and everyone knew his or her role. In reality, however, the truly "good old days" of the Church were Christ's three public years and the apostolic era which followed the first Pentecost. That's when Christ's words and deeds were fresh and the Spirit was exploding in the minds and hearts of Christ's disciples.

But we know that the Catholic Church has undergone enormous, radical changes since the first century A.D. and certainly has experienced great changes since the Second Vatican Council. Most notably, the concept of ministry in the post-Vatican II era is much different from that which prevailed before the watershed decade of the 1960s. No longer is the priest one of very few highly educated members of the community; no longer can pastors rule parishes as fiefdoms or benevolent dictatorships. The operative phrase in today's Church is "collaborative ministry." For reasons too numerous to explore here, ordained clergy, professed religious, and confirmed laity are coalescing into leadership and decision-making associations in parishes and dioceses throughout the United States. Stewardship conversion takes root and flourishes where every ministry is valued, where everyone's gifts of time and talent are appreciated, and where each parishioner assumes ownership of his or her parish and diocese.

Listen, once again, to the U.S. bishops in their pastoral letter on stewardship:

> Because its individual members do collectively make up the Body of Christ, that body's health and well-being are...the personal responsibility of each one of us. We all are stewards of the Church... stewardship in an ecclesial setting means cherishing and fostering the gifts of all, while using one's own gifts to serve the community of faith...Those who set their hearts upon spiritual gifts must "seek to have an abundance for building up the church" (1 Cor 14:12). But how is the Church built up? In a sense there are as many answers to that question as there are individual members with individual vocations. But the overarching answer for all is this: through personal participation in and support of the Church's mission of proclaiming and teaching, serving and sanctifying. This participa-

tion takes different forms according to people's different gifts and offices, but there is a fundamental obligation arising from the sacrament of baptism that people place their gifts, their resources—their selves—at God's service in and through the Church.

One of the great struggles for today's Christians is to hold fast to eternal, immutable truths and faith dogmas in a world that is in perpetual motion around us! Our anchor in this stormy sea of change must be Jesus Christ. And, as faithful disciples of Jesus, we must constantly revitalize our commitment to a stewardship way of life.

2. STEWARDSHIP OF TIME

Think about it: what is more dear to us than our time? Not diamonds, not gold, not stocks and bonds, and certainly not money, which we never seem to have enough of anyway! Not even parents, children, or friends can be counted as more important because without our time, we would not be able to enjoy and love them.

We are very protective of our time. In fact, the older we become, the more protective we are, perhaps because, with age, we grow increasingly aware of the limited amount of earthly time we have. As people of faith, we believe that time is simply a way to measure God's great gift of life. Furthermore, as disciples of Jesus Christ, we are aware of our obligation to be good stewards of our time and, indeed, of all the blessings God has bestowed on us. Among other things, this means giving back to God, in gratitude, a portion of our time to help build God's kingdom on earth.

In the real world of sleeping, eating, working, and doing other "stuff," how much time do we have to return to God? Let's review the numbers: There are 8,760 hours in a 365-day year. If we sleep an average of 8 hours a day (unrealistic for workaholics; totally unacceptable for teenagers), we reduce our conscious hours by 2,920 annually, leaving 5,840.

Working outside the home for a traditional 40 hours per week for 50 weeks—don't forget the 2-week vacation!—reduces the time over which we have more or less conscious control by 2,000 hours, leaving 3,840. (NOTE: we won't even attempt to calculate the untold number of hours stay-at-home parents of small children must spend on their chores!) If we factor in a one-hour commute to and from work (a half-hour each way, which would be nirvana for residents of many large metro areas!), we are left with 3,590 hours. Now let's throw in 2 hours a day for meals and 1 hour a day for personal grooming, which may be inadequate for some. The result is 2,495 hours which we might call our "disposable time."

Let's take a closer look at this disposable time. Most people watch television; so, for the purposes of this exercise, let's assume we watch an average of 2 hours of television each day (for example, a half-hour of national news, a half-hour of local news, and an hour of other programming). We have now reduced our annual allotment of spendable hours to about 6 or 7 hours a day to do things like shopping, hobbies, shuttling kids to soccer, visiting relatives and friends, napping, doing laundry, paying bills, going to church, and so on.

Why is it, with all the timesaving devices available to us, we still seem to have less and less time on our hands? In some cases it's the fault of the very devices which are supposed to "save time!" Electronic and technological gadgets may actually eat up large chunks of time, as anyone who has "surfed the Internet" or tried to speak to a living person at the other end of the telephone line can attest.

How we choose to share our time is a personal study in setting priorities, and is generally our response to such questions as: What do I feel obligated to do? What do I want to do? What do I like to do? What gives me some return on my time investment? Am I recognized for my efforts? Are my efforts appreciated?

Parishes that conduct annual stewardship renewals (see Chapters 4 and 13) notice that the response to stewardship of treasure renewals (that is, increased financial giving) is proportionately much greater than the response to time and talent renewals. Why? Because it's easier for many (most?) parishioners to write a bigger check each week than it is to give more of their time and talent to the programs and services offered by the parish.

The premier stewardship of time and talent challenge for a parish engaged in stewardship conversion is to figure out ways to "bump" parish needs to the top of parishioners' priority lists! Remember, we are always competing with the "business of busyness," that is, the perception by many people that they have precious little time to spare. In most cases, however, the real task is determining how to help parishioners understand the difference between "doing the job right" and "doing the right job"!

3. STEWARDSHIP OF TALENT

Through a unique and mysterious confluence of genetics and environment, one person paints masterpieces, another writes epics, another composes symphonies, while still others run faster, jump higher, or grow stronger than ordinary humans. To be sure, hard work, dedication, and personal effort are often required to develop one's native talents; but, we Christians profess to believe that the basic psychological and physiological traits from which extraordinary performances and accomplishments flow are originally unearned gifts from God.

The heart and soul of Christian stewardship is the belief that God is the Source of all our blessings and possessions. We own nothing. We are simply God's stewards. During our earthly sojourn, we are allowed temporary use of God's property. According to Christ's words, God expects us to be responsible and accountable stewards. And God expects some reasonable return on this investment as a token of our gratitude. Returning time, talent, and treasure to God has been described as "taking our hands off some of God's possessions."

As we focus on our God-given talents, we will consider three issues: (a) identifying and "owning" talents, (b) matching talents to needs, and (c) determining what talents to return to God.

A. Identifying and Owning Talents

Before we can gratefully return a portion of our talents to God, we must first identify and "own" them. How often do we hear people say: "Oh, I have no particular talents," or "I'm not good at (insert any ability or skill here); I just try hard." In a world frequently subjected to braggarts and blowhards, self-effacing humility can be a welcome relief. However, God does not breathe a life into us that is totally devoid of abilities, skills, talents, and interests. Saint Paul was absolutely correct: "For as in one body we have many members, and not all the members have the same function, so we, who are many, are one body in Christ, and individually we are members one of another. We have gifts that differ according to the grace given us" (Rom 12:4-6). Everyone receives a unique array of God's gifts. The challenge for disciples of Jesus Christ is to discover our gifts, develop them, and return a portion to God in gratitude.

Here are some questions which individuals and organizations can use to provoke personal inventories of talents, skills, and abilities:

1. What is my occupation, vocation, or profession?
2. What additional skills, talents, or interests do I have?
3. What are my hobbies? What do I like to do in my spare time?
4. What skills or talents do I have because of my hobbies?

5. What kinds of skills, talents, or abilities do my friends and family members tell me I have?
6. What are some specific needs in my community that I know I could help meet?

Discovering our talents is not a one-time exercise; it's a process that changes as we reach new developmental stages in our lives.

Some Catholics have difficulty acknowledging their talents. Many of us were taught at an early age not to flaunt our abilities; to do so would be a sin of pride. Yet we have repeatedly heard Christ's admonition: "No one after lighting a lamp puts it under the bushel basket, but on the lampstand, and it gives light to all in the house. In the same way, let your light shine before others, so that they may see your good works and give glory to your Father in heaven" (Mt 5:15–16). Parish leaders may have to help some parishioners learn that it's okay to acknowledge, indeed, be rightfully proud of, the special gifts God has entrusted to their care.

B. Matching Talents to Needs

How often do parish leaders say: "It's always the same people in this parish who do everything. Why can't we get more folks involved?" The answer to this question may require a complete overhaul of a parish's entire volunteer recruitment system and leadership style. If, for example, "We've always done it this way" is the title of the parish council's theme song, it doesn't take great insight to diagnose the problem. Even parishes that profess to be welcoming, hospitable communities can inadvertently become controlled by a destructive status quo or clique mentality. If, for another example, a parish is governed from the top down by means of inflexible leadership, only the most tolerant and long-suffering parishioners will have the stamina to become involved.

If, however, a parish has initiated a stewardship conversion process, one of its goals must be to attract every parishioner into active participation in the life of the parish family. Astute parish leaders already know that many people are not assertive, step-forward joiners: they must somehow be invited to become more involved. Reluctance to volunteer is a common human reaction among people who, for a variety of reasons, feel unsure of themselves or who don't believe they have anything worthwhile to contribute. A skillful parish leadership team can help irresolute parishioners overturn their bushel baskets and liberate their lights.

Many parishioners may not see the connection between their skills and abilities, and parish needs. One way of engaging reluctant parishioners is to provide them with a means to assess their own talents and interests. This assessment, if properly developed and promoted, can direct parishioners toward the types of parish ministries, services, and programs they will find rewarding and satisfying. An example of such an assessment can be found in Appendix 2: "Time and Talent Renewals: Sample Materials."

A second method of attracting parishioners into more active involvement is by fostering a "can't-say-no" attitude. This strategy was discovered by the pastor of a very successful stewardship parish who, when asked to disclose his secret for engaging so many parishioners, responded: "When someone approaches me with an idea for a new group, or new program or new service for the parish, my answer is always the same: 'Find a few more folks who are interested in the same idea and go ahead with it.' Why should I get in a person's way who is trying to draw closer to God? If starting this club or that organization will help my people feel more welcome and involved in our parish, why should I say no?"

A can't-say-no parish disposition tells uninvolved or marginally active parishioners that they are free to create ways to meet their own needs as they help the parish grow and prosper. They don't need to wait for staff members to dictate what must be done. For their part, parish staff members must trust the Holy Spirit to muster and energize the collective wisdom and talent of parishioners. There's always more than one way to reach a goal or accomplish a task.

Another means of helping parishioners match their skills and interests with parish needs is by developing and publishing job descriptions. These can be either generic or task-specific, or both. A generic job description for liturgical ministries (lectors, musicians, servers, and so on) might look like this:

Liturgical ministers

- Love prayer and celebration
- Are happy in gatherings of people
- Are committed to community worship
- Enjoy positive, uplifting church liturgies and preparing for feasts and liturgical seasons
- Want to hear, spread, and live the Word of God
- Have good "people skills" and are willing to be in the public eye

A specific job description for lectors might include these elements:

Lectors
- pleasant, strong voice
- punctual and dependable
- ability to read aloud intelligibly with feeling and conviction
- willing to rehearse and participate in diocesan lector-training program
- pleasant, presentable demeanor
- available to be scheduled for at least two weekend Masses each month

C. Determining What Talents to Return to God

Unlike time and money, talents are difficult to quantify and therefore do not easily lend themselves to a strict application of the concept of tithing. However, as one becomes increasingly aware of his or her abilities, Christ's words begin to make even more sense: "Much will be required; and from everyone to whom much has been given and from the one to whom much has been entrusted, even more will be demanded" (Lk 12:48).

What does it mean to give "more talents?" Perhaps it has to do with the amount of risk, the level of intensity, the degree of difficulty, the magnitude of sacrifice, none of which can be measured in dollars and cents or by a clock, but are certainly known by the steward who gives them. The person who struggles to give three hours a week to clean the church may be giving the same amount of talent back to God as is the person who spends three hours a month in meetings as a member of the parish council. Yet, in all cases, the grateful return of talents to God should always be emotionally enriching and spiritually satisfying for the giver.

CHAPTER 2

The Big Three

Parish and diocesan leaders who are responsible for fostering stewardship conversion among Catholic Christians need to recognize and thank the visionary pioneers whose efforts in the final quarter of the twentieth century paved the way. One trail-blazing community is St. Francis of Assisi Parish in Wichita, Kansas, under the prophetic leadership of its now-retired pastor, Msgr. Thomas McGread.

The story of St. Francis of Assisi's stewardship journey has been documented many times elsewhere and is, in fact, available directly from the parish (see Chapter 20: "References and Resources"). The basis for St. Francis's achievements can be summarized in three words which capture the essence of a total-stewardship parish: prayer, hospitality, and service.

1. PRAYER

The prayer life of a total-stewardship parish *must* be rooted in the celebration of the holy Eucharist. The Mass is the parish family gathered to worship and praise God, to publicly witness its stewardship of time, talent, and treasure, and to be nourished and sustained through Christ's body and blood in its efforts to live as a family of good stewards. Because weekend liturgies are occasions when most members of a congregation come together, parish leaders must use these opportunities judiciously.

Patrick McNamara and Charles Zech recently reported on the factors that impact positively on the stewardship conversion process. In the September 14, 1996, issue of *America* magazine, these researchers indicate that excellent homilies—which necessarily entail impressive liturgies—contribute mightily to the success of a parish's stewardship reformation. They go on to write: "...our case studies show...(that) well-managed Catholic parishes...are characterized by financial openness, *participation in a liturgy that is vital*, accessibility of both pastor and staff and vibrant ministries that parishioners are encouraged to start up and participate in."

Further, Francis Scheets and Joseph Harris, in another article in *America* (July 15, 1995), comment thusly: "We have noted that Catholic contributions tend to be much lower than Protestant contributions....What encourages Catholics to increase their Sunday contributions?...The major factors that encouraged or discouraged donors were: *effectiveness in preaching*, in pastoral visits and in staff community leadership; further, open discussion of parish decisions, good morale, and the extent to which a majority of parishioners are actively involved."

Good liturgies don't just happen; they result from careful planning. Well-prepared liturgies ensure inspiring homilies, spiritually uplifting music, and engaging celebrations which, in turn, stimulate active participation by the congregation during Mass, to be continued later beyond church walls. Efficacious liturgies are the wellspring from which flows the prayer-streams that course through the life of the parish community.

2. HOSPITALITY

A total-stewardship parish is a welcoming place: its members feel that they belong and are appreciated. Parish staff and parishioners work tirelessly to create a spirited parish family, not just an association of strangers. If asked to express their affiliation to the parish, each parishioner would quickly respond: "This is my parish. Its success or failure depends on me."

Listen once again to what McNamara and Zech report: "Leadership challenges in Catholic parishes...*include imparting to congregations a sense of ownership, that the church 'belongs to them.'* As one East Coast pastor put it, 'I think among Catholics you're going to have difficulty increasing the giving if you convey the thought that the church belongs to the priest. The moment you say that the church belongs to the people, they will listen to you.' Another pastor remarked in the same article: "Parishes where people do have ownership are more vital, more alive parishes. In organizations where people have a sense of ownership and know their input is important, they are going to give time and financial backing."

A hospitable parish is not just a place where people go; it's also a place where Christians want to be. Parish leaders promote and model hospitality each time parishioners gather, no matter how large or small the group. Meeting and gathering spaces are well prepared and fully equipped; appropriate refreshments are served; punctuality is expected. Furthermore, hospitality is not the responsibility only of those who may be designated "greeters" or hosts and hostesses for parish celebrations and other events. Each member understands his or her personal obligation to be welcoming and hospitable to guests and fellow parishioners alike.

3. SERVICE

Next to one's own blood family, a total-stewardship parish stands ready to minister to its parishioners. Wherever and whenever its members are hurting or in need, or celebrating and giving thanks, or seeking salvation, or wanting to return to God a portion of their God-given gifts, all of these needs and more are met within the total-stewardship parish.

It's a comfort to observe a stewardship parish family wrap its collective arms around one of its members who is suffering or in need of help. It's a delight when a parish family rejoices and celebrates special events and milestones in its members' lives. Conversely, it's sad when Christians deliberately alienate themselves from the spiritual safety net a stewardship parish is always ready to extend to them.

We must remember that the level of service that most parishioners now anticipate has advanced beyond former standards. The U.S. business community has been steadily raising the quality-of-service bar for several years, thanks, in part, to fierce competition and modeling from foreign companies. American consumers now expect world-class service; in the business world, it's referred to as "value-added service." Customer service researchers Karl Albrecht and Ron Zemke, in their book *Service America* (Homewood, Ill.: Dow Jones-Irwin, 1985) describe it this way:

> Value-added service is more easily understood in experience than in definition; you know it when you see it. Because a cabin attendant pushing the drink wagon on Republic 507 out of Chicago is out of loose change, she gives you back three one-dollar bills from a five for a $2.50 drink. In response to an offhand comment you made, a calling officer from Wachovia Bank and Trust, who pitched factoring services to you last week, sends you an article on how to use limited trusts to help put your kids through college. A 3M visual-products representative setting up a seminar on how to use

overhead projectors in sales presentations stays to help one of your salespeople rehearse for a next-day presentation. All those people are practicing the fine art of value-added service (pages 7-8).

A total-stewardship parish needs to understand that these are the criteria against which parishioners will measure the service they receive, the parish programs they attend, and activities in which they participate!

CHAPTER 3

Volunteers: The Organizational Drive Shaft

It takes many things to make a parish, school, diocese, or other Catholic institution function efficiently and effectively: professional staff, funds, equipment, and supplies, to name just a few. Using an admittedly trite automotive metaphor, the paid professional staff is the engine, money is fuel and lubrication, office equipment and supplies are support parts like the frame, fuel pump, tires, radiator, and so on. If, however, all of these components are working in perfect harmony, our organizational car will still not move without one final, essential piece of hardware: the drive shaft.

The drive shaft for almost every nonprofit organization is its priceless and faithful corps of volunteers. Volunteers transfer the power generated by the staff engine and budget fuel to the wheels so the organization can fulfill its mission.

In a Catholic parish, for example, volunteers provide the creative energy and muscle needed to extend and perform parish services and ministries. Without their selfless gifts of time and talent, the spirit of the community would wither and die. Therefore, the proper care and treatment of volunteers should be required skills for leaders of Catholic parishes and organizations. Why? Because the future of the U.S. Catholic Church hangs in the balance! In addition to permanent deacons, religious, and laity who are accepting professional leadership positions in parishes and schools, the growing shortage of priests is generating a need for laypeople to assume more parish ownership and involvement as volunteers.

It's no secret that seminary experiences and theological education in years past were noticeably inadequate regarding much of the human, real-world "stuff" young priests encountered following ordination. This included almost no attention paid to the abilities and information needed to implement stewardship conversion initiatives in the parishes to which they were assigned, and no well-conceived "people-skills" training programs for leading and managing employees and volunteers. The jury is still out regarding the treatment of these topics in today's seminary programs.

In this section, we will take a brief look at the core disciplines and issues that relate to working with volunteers. Christian volunteers are, after all, stewards who are returning to God a portion of their God-given gifts of time and talent through parish and community service involvement; most nonprofit organizations could not survive without them.

1. WHAT IS A VOLUNTEER?

A volunteer is a person who, of his or her own free will, offers himself or herself for a service or duty. An even simpler definition is: someone who chooses to work without pay. The fact that volunteers are not paid immediately demonstrates their value for a parish or other organization, but also suggests several problems and concerns we will consider later.

2. WHAT IS A GOOD VOLUNTEER?

Volunteers, like paid employees, come with all manners of abilities and attitudes. When Brad Butler, former Vice Chairman of Proctor & Gamble, was asked what P&G looked for in an entry level employee, his answer was simple and straightforward: "We need someone who can read, write, and speak effectively...and respond to an alarm clock!" Anyone whose projects or activities require the use of volunteers would probably echo Mr. Butler's words if asked what they look for in a good volunteer.

There are three principal attributes of an ideal volunteer: (a) reliability, (b) fit, and (c) commitment.

A. Reliability

Most parish leaders would probably agree that the most valued trait of volunteers is reliability: they show up when they say they will, they're on time, and they're ready to complete their assignment!

B. Fit

When a volunteer's skills, abilities, interests, and personality closely correspond to the requirements of the task to be performed, everybody wins. A well-matched volunteer is happy, easy to motivate, productive, cooperative, and a true complement to an organization's paid professional staff. Staff members are delighted to have volunteers upon whom they can rely to support their work and the organization's mission.

A parish receives both human and financial benefits from volunteers' gifts of time and talent. The morale of paid employees is bolstered by competent, enthusiastic volunteers, and there is an obvious budgetary savings when volunteers can assume responsibility for a portion of the parish workload. A mismatched volunteer, on the other hand, will be an unhappy volunteer who will often cause grief for paid employees and other volunteers.

C. Commitment

Top-quality volunteers are those who feel ownership for their parishes and their assignments. They find joy in their duties, no matter how menial. They are team players who are eager to help; but, more than that, they want to do a good job and will do whatever it takes to get the job done. Their spirited dedication makes them easy to supervise.

There is one major danger regarding the best volunteers: staff members may take advantage of their devotion and overuse them. The consequence is volunteer burnout. Parishes that rely heavily on volunteers must constantly monitor scheduling and assignment rosters to be sure staff members are not inadvertently expecting too much of their volunteers.

3. THE PARISH VOLUNTEER PROGRAM

You may have noticed by now that expectations placed on volunteers are similar to those placed on any good, paid employee. One major difference is that parish leaders generally feel they have less control over volunteers, and therefore can put fewer demands on them because they are not financially compensated for their labors. Supervision of volunteers does require leadership skills and management techniques somewhat different from those needed to oversee paid employees.

Responses to the following two questions can provide the foundation for a parish's philosophy regarding the oversight of volunteers:

1. How do parish leaders, particularly paid staff, view volunteers?
2. How do volunteers see their role within the parish?

Paid employees may answer the first question with a range of answers from a high-end "essential to parish life" to a low-end "necessary evil." Volunteers's responses to the second question would probably cover a spectrum ranging from a high of "laborer of love" to a low of "unpaid employee." The goal of every parish is to insure that its volunteer program elicits the high-end answers.

There are four major topics that must be included in a discussion of the development and maintenance of a systematic parish volunteer program: (a) recruitment, (b) supervision, (c) motivation, and (d) redirection.

A. Recruitment

Acquiring volunteers involves several phases and procedures including:

Who should ask? Since most people are not "joiners" by nature, it's necessary to develop strategies to determine who would be the best persons in the parish to ask fellow parishioners to volunteer for specific ministries or tasks.

How are people asked? Depending on the ministry, program or service needing assistance, different techniques for asking people to volunteer may be required. Sometimes a general call for volunteers utilizing sign-up sheets is sufficient. At other times, a personal invitation is the most appropriate means.

Expectations/job descriptions: One of the most helpful tools in recruiting volunteers is a written job description for the task(s) to be performed. In addition to a detailed explanation of the job, it should include an estimate of the time that will be required, a general overview of the skills and abilities required, and review of any training that might be necessary.

Screening/selection: No one who volunteers for every task is the appropriate person. Someone should be given the responsibility to determine if a volunteer's skills and interests fit the job to be performed, and to help all volunteers match their abilities to parish needs.

B. Supervision

A well-conceived parish volunteer program includes clearly delineated lines of authority for management and supervision. The elements which fall under this heading include:

Training: Nothing contributes more to early dissatisfaction and frustration—and quick burnout—than volunteering for a task for which there is no orientation or preparation. Even the most menial jobs should include a training component; it's simply a matter of courtesy toward volunteering parishioners, and respect for their desire to return to God a portion of their gifts.

Coordinating/Scheduling: In general, paid staff members should coordinate and schedule most volunteer activities. In addition, volunteers should know whom to contact at the parish office when they have questions.

Communication: Where needed, communication vehicles should be developed and utilized so that volunteers and potential volunteers are regularly and properly informed about available opportunities, scheduled events, and so on.

Support: This element includes making sure volunteers have space to meet, materials and equipment to perform their chosen tasks, hospitable amenities when appropriate, and a designated "go-to person" when problems arise.

C. Motivation

Discovering Volunteers' Hot Buttons: Top-notch volunteer programs include an often-overlooked component devoted to helping volunteers discover their talents, skills, and interests. Many parishioners may have to be gently nudged to recognize and disclose their good qualities and abilities. Several techniques can be employed for this purpose including paper and pencil inventories and personal interviews. Qualified staff members or trained volunteers may also conduct small group "self-discovery mini-retreats" as an avenue for personal exploration.

Motivational Tools: When employees are asked to name and rank the things they want most from their jobs, one item invariably tops the list: "Full appreciation of work done." Nothing motivates people more than gratitude. Volunteers are no different from paid staff in this regard. The most powerful motivational tool in a parish leader's toolbox is a frequent, well-placed "thank you." It's deceptively easy for busy bosses and supervisors to take employees and volunteers for granted and fail to express their appreciation.

Thanking volunteers in a parish setting can take many forms:

- Public recognition at the close of Mass or during special parish celebrations
- Items in parish bulletins or newsletters
- Handwritten notes from the pastor or parish leaders
- A "walk-through" by key staff members during a particular event or activity with appropriate expressions of approval and gratitude
- Well-organized and publicized ministry days
- Commissioning services during weekend Masses

Enlist the creativity of the community to add to this list.

D. Redirection

Volunteers occasionally burn out, or they are mismatched with their tasks, or they do not work well with paid staff members or other volunteers. At these times, it's necessary for them to be "redirected." Precisely because they are volunteers, dismissal usually doesn't fit the circumstances. As one harried pastor said: "How can I fire a volunteer?" Redirection, as the term implies, involves exploring other available tasks with volunteers and offering them alternatives.

The goal of redirection is to help volunteers maintain their self-esteem and commitment to the parish while moving toward responsibilities for which their abilities and personalities are better suited. This requires gentle yet resolute sensitivity and involves skillful coaching and counseling techniques, not accusatory confrontation or personal attacks. Conversations should be laced with positive encouragement and focus on observable, measurable behaviors and factual data.

Redirection should be conducted by a recognized parish leader who has the proper skills. The key phrase is "proper skills." Many parish leaders have not been trained to deal with the multiple personnel issues that arise in today's increasingly complex parish environment. Advanced "people skills" training for parish leaders should be a priority.

Some effective redirection strategies are

- Reassess the volunteer's skills and abilities
- Conduct an inventory of his or her interests
- Offer advanced training and/or mentoring
- Review alternative parish programs and services which match the volunteers' talents and wishes

4. THE DIRECTOR OF VOLUNTEERISM

As parishioners become more involved in the life of a stewardship parish community, there's an almost relentless increase in the number of new programs and services as well as greater participation in existing activities. This increased participation puts more demands on pastors and other staff members. Consequently, a stewardship parish might want to consider adding a Director of Volunteerism to its staff. Depending on parish size and resources, this could be either full time or part time, paid or volunteer.

The Director of Volunteerism (DOV) is a staff member at the same level as a Pastoral Associate, Parish Business Manager, or School Principal. The DOV manages every aspect of parish volunteer activity, from basic organizing and scheduling to advanced training and recruiting, and renders whatever assistance and education volunteer groups need to conduct their business, provide their services, or complete their projects. (See sample DOV job description in Appendix 10.)

By adding a professional Director of Volunteerism to its administrative mix, a parish makes a powerful statement about the strength of its commitment to stewardship conversion.

CHAPTER 4

Time and Talent Renewals

A stewardship renewal is a designated span of time—usually three to five weeks—during which a parish focuses an extraordinary amount of resources and energy on the stewardship conversion process and education about the stewardship way of life. During the renewal period, every possible means of communication is used to instruct parishioners about their responsibilities as disciples of Jesus Christ, and to motivate them to accept a more intense commitment to a stewardship attitude in mind and heart. As the renewal period reaches its culmination, parishioners are invited to declare their revitalized affirmation of stewardship by filling out some type of commitment or intent card.

The ideal stewardship renewal agenda incorporates all three stewardship "T's": time, talent, and treasure. However, because the specific elements of time and talent renewals are slightly different from treasure renewals, and because, for certain pastoral and practical reasons, some parish leaders choose to renew time and talent separately from treasure, we will discuss them separately. A discussion of stewardship of treasure renewals can be found in Chapter 13.

1. COMPONENTS

A few dioceses and several publishing and fund-raising consulting companies have developed parish stewardship renewal programs that include standard packets of materials and supplies. Here are the recommended ingredients for a competent stewardship of time and talent renewal package:

- Calendar of events and activities
- Bulletin inserts
- Letters from the pastor and/or other parish leader(s)
- Newsletter articles
- Promotional clip art
- Prayers of the faithful
- Stewardship homily ideas
- Posters
- List of time and talent opportunities
- Time and talent offering card (sign-up form)
- Treasure commitment form (optional)
- Return address envelopes ("business reply" preferred)

Examples of some of the items listed above can be found in Appendix 2.

2. FREQUENCY AND TIMING

Stewardship conversion experts generally recommend that stewardship renewals take place at least once a year. Parishes with highly mobile memberships may need even more frequent renewal periods. Smaller parishes may require less frequent renewals. When time and talent renewals are conducted separately from treasure renewals, an alternating schedule is recommended, either annually or every six months.

There is no definitive "best time" for conducting renewals. However, a parish should make every effort to clear its docket so that no other major project intrudes on the renewal's activities. Stewardship renewals tend to fit well into the seasons of Lent and Advent because of their timing and spiritual themes. In other words, the ideal time to conduct a stewardship renewal is any time a parish can devote maximum energy and attention to the stewardship way of life.

A word of caution: As already noted, stewardship conversion flourishes when a stewardship attitude becomes part of the fabric of parish life. Parish leaders must not mistake occasional stewardship renewal periods for the ongoing process of stewardship conversion promoted in this book. Stewardship renewals are but one item on the stewardship conversion menu; they are indeed useful and necessary, but they should not be viewed as a substitute for year-round thematic emphasis on stewardship as a way of life.

3. PITFALLS AND POSITIVES

Here's a practical review of stewardship renewal issues and tips under the headings "pitfalls" and "positives":

Pitfalls: These are items and circumstances which could minimize the overall effectiveness of an otherwise adequate stewardship of time and talent renewal:

- *"Sign-up" system that causes inappropriate volunteering.* Asking parishioners to volunteer for only one or two ministries or activities, or to rank their choices, can create difficulties when the choices do not match parishioners' skills and abilities.
  TIP: Ask parishioners to select "at least three but not more than five programs or projects." Then add: "We will ask you to serve where you are needed most."
- *Materials that are unattractive, hard to read, and not "user-friendly."*
  TIP: Solicit feedback from several parishioners about all renewal materials before "going to press." Be sure type styles are easy to read, particularly for older parishioners. Test instructions to see if they are convenient and easy to follow.
- *Forgetting the children.* Children can have a powerful influence on their families in matters of faith.
  TIP: Involve DRE's, CRE's and Catholic school faculties in the design and implementation of each renewal. Be sure to coordinate all religious education programs with the renewal agenda.
- *Creating a "junk-mail" scenario.* Great care should be taken that materials mailed to parishioners are not perceived as junk mail, thereby subject to immediate dismissal!
  TIP: Personalize and sign every letter; print addresses directly on envelopes (no labels!); affix "live" first-class stamps (no bulk mail).
- *No immediate follow-up.* Without exception, the most disastrous faux pas for time and talent renewals is not contacting parishioners immediately after their commitment forms have been returned.

TIP: Long before the stewardship renewal begins, be sure that those who are responsible for every ministry or service have a definite plan for contacting parishioners who volunteer for their respective groups within one week after commitment forms have been returned.

Positives: Here are a few observations and practical tips to improve renewal efforts and help assess their results:

- Give current volunteers permission to change ministries without feeling guilty or disloyal.
- Plan all liturgies during the renewal period around stewardship themes.
- During renewal periods, work harder than usual to create and maintain a welcoming, hospitable atmosphere throughout the parish.
- Take every opportunity to praise and thank parishioners for their past generosity and service, and celebrate their willingness to demonstrate even greater compassion and commitment.
- Use a self-assessment instrument which helps parishioners identify their gifts and interests prior to filling out their commitment forms.
- Employ every available medium to publicize and promote the renewal period: newsletters, announcements at meetings, posters, bulletin inserts, prayers of the faithful, homilies, religious education programs, and so on.
- During the renewal period, minimize all possible distractions. Don't schedule renewals during high liturgical seasons or at times which may conflict with special parish celebrations such as first Communions, confirmations, graduations, and so on.
- Use lay witnesses as much as possible.

Parishes that conduct time/talent and treasure renewals separately will notice a marked disparity in their response rate (that is, the percentage of offering or commitment cards that are completed and returned to the parish). Experience has shown that stewardship of treasure renewals tend to generate a significantly higher return than time and talent renewals because most people today seem to be more protective of their time than their money.

4. THE MINISTRY FAIR

A Ministry Fair is an outstanding way to recognize and thank volunteers for their generous gifts of time and talents, as well as showcase parish ministries, programs and organizations. It's also a marvelous vehicle for soliciting new volunteers and members.

In her excellent reference manual, *How to Present a Ministry Fair* (Kansas City, Mo.: Sheed & Ward, 1996), author Rita McCarthy Swartz writes:

> The Ministry Fair is a once-a-year celebration of the participation, contributions, and importance of the work of parish ministry. It allows all members to recognize with pride the value provided by the parish through its volunteer efforts. The fair is a method of focusing attention on the stewardship of time and talent and educating parishioners on the importance of giving (page 2).

According to Swartz, a successful ministry fair requires these elements:

- A series of mailings to parish ministry leadership to plan and evaluate the event, and to parish members with information about parish ministries.
- Time and talent activities such as a parade of ministry banners, display tables, sign-ups after Mass, and a giving tree.
- Time and talent presentations by the pastor and lay witnesses.

Swartz's booklet includes specific instructions and examples of each component necessary for a ministry fair (see the Bibliography on page 213).

Parishes that conduct ministry fairs should invite stewardship committees from other parishes to visit their events for two reasons: (1) to share creative ideas and resources; and (2) to solicit constructive feedback. Some diocesan offices serve as a central repository for parish ministry fair schedules and other local stewardship-related events.

5. PARISH MISSIONS AND RENEWALS

From time to time, many parishes hold what are variously called "parish missions" or "parish renewals" in conjunction with stewardship renewals, or to supplement their stewardship conversion processes. Parish missions are generally short (one-week), intense programs led by a guest director or team skilled in making inspirational, motivational presentations. Parishioners attend a series of evening events conducted by the visiting director or team. With proper follow-through, a parish mission can be a powerful "booster shot" for stewardship conversion.

Parish renewals are typically longer formal programs (sometimes one or two years) built around an elaborate system of small group development activities. Examples of these programs are "Christ Renews His Parish" and "Renew." Such programs, when incorporated into a parish's commitment to a stewardship way of life, can also benefit the conversion process.

CHAPTER 5

The Stewardship Committee

Conventional wisdom, coupled with a mountain of experience, suggests that stewardship conversion should be directed by people who are committed to a stewardship way of life, and who are widely respected members of the community. These are the kinds of Christians who should be invited to serve on parish and diocesan stewardship committees.

For many pastoral leaders, committees are a bane; they can create headaches and roadblocks that didn't exist when parishes were run by pastoral autocrats or benevolent dictators. But the days when pastors made every major parish decision are virtually extinct. Today's church leaders are struggling to adjust to new leadership paradigms based on techniques such as consensus-building, discernment, participatory leadership, collaborative ministries, and the principle of subsidiarity, along with the joys and miseries that accompany them.

Committees can indeed be exasperating gatherings which impede progress rather than promote it. On the other hand, committees can be a true blessing. When properly constructed, they place a wealth of experiences and knowledge in the meeting room. And, if facilitated by people trained in the art of conducting efficient, productive meetings, they can be fountains of creativity and powerful change-agents.

1. QUALITIES OF MEMBERS

Who should be asked to serve on a stewardship committee? To answer this question, we turn to a parish already renowned as one of the most prosperous stewardship parishes in the United States: St. Francis of Assisi in Wichita, Kansas. Here's an excerpt from St. Francis's own parish stewardship handbook entitled *Stewardship: Living Life As God Intended.*

> A good place to begin the (stewardship committee) selection process is the front of the church. Our experience at St. Francis has taught us that the people most committed to stewardship are Eucharistic people, daily communicants in many cases. Those people in your parish most likely to possess the enthusiasm, the energy, the deep belief necessary to win others to a new way of life will draw their strength from the Lord's Body and Blood. Parishioners who fully appreciate the magnitude of Jesus' daily gift of Himself will fully appreciate the debt we owe in return (page 5).

Desirable stewardship committee candidates are "doers" who like to finish what they start. They are respected by their fellow parishioners as good stewards. They should also be people of vision capable of sharing a common dream and working with others. Above all, they should be people of prayer who are unshakable in their faith and dedicated disciples of Jesus Christ.

2. SELECTION PROCESS

Stewardship committees should be hand-picked by parish and diocesan leaders. The number of members partly depends on the size of the organization. For example, ten to sixteen members would be a suitable working group for medium-to-large parishes; smaller parishes may operate well with six to eight member committees. Married members should be asked to serve as couples since committee members will undoubtedly experience personal changes in lifestyles and value systems as they deepen their commitment to stewardship. Member-couples also add a bonus to stewardship committees. If one spouse is occasionally unable to attend a meeting, the other can keep him or her up-to-date.

Committee members should be asked to serve a minimum term of three years for two principal reasons:

- *Continuity:* Frequent turnover will interfere with the development of close relationships among members and can seriously disrupt morale as well as the committee's programs and projects.
- *Success experiences:* Stewardship conversion is a process which unfolds over time. In its early stages, the process may move slowly. Committee members should stay involved long enough to experience success as a result of their efforts. In most cases, committee members are welcome to remain on the committee as long as they wish beyond their initial three-year commitment. Experience shows that most members remain active for several additional years.

3. SAMPLE RESPONSIBILITIES

Each parish has its own corporate personality. When it embarks on a stewardship conversion journey, that personality plays a major role in determining what types of stewardship-related programs and services are needed. It is, therefore, impossible to formulate a universally applicable, lockstep itinerary of fixed projects for stewardship committees to use. We can, however, suggest particular activities and programs that most active parish stewardship committees tend to utilize. When to employ any or all of the following depends on where the parish is located on its path to total stewardship:

- Conduct annual periods of stewardship renewal (see Chapters 4 and 13)
- Prepare and maintain a parish directory (see Chapter 7)
- Identify and help train parishioners who are willing to share their personal stewardship stories with fellow parishioners (see Chapter 8)
- Provide for prompt follow-up of stewardship of time and talent sign-ups resulting from renewals or parish ministry days
- Organize parish ministry fairs (see Chapter 4)
- Establish and conduct an annual evaluation of the effectiveness of stewardship-related programs and projects
- Oversee the production and distribution of a parish newsletter (see Chapter 6)
- Publish stewardship thoughts in each issue of the parish bulletin and newsletter

- Make appropriate stewardship literature available in parish booklet racks
- Incorporate comments about stewardship in weekend homilies
- Encourage support for stewardship through the prayers of the faithful at Mass
- Develop a comprehensive welcoming and hospitality program for parishioners and visitors
- Expand the focus of stewardship beyond parish boundaries

4. TRAINING/PREPARATION/SUPPORT

When a parish organizes its first stewardship committee, parish leaders must remember that committee members will need a strong dose of self-assurance. A formal preservice training component is vital, not only to bolster the committee's confidence but also to ensure the committee's success.

A primary resource for parishes seeking help as they form stewardship committees are diocesan offices of stewardship and/or development. Most have, or have access to, stewardship conversion materials and information. Many diocesan offices also provide training and consulting services for parish stewardship needs, and a growing number of dioceses conduct annual "stewardship days" featuring guest speakers and workshops designed to educate parishioners about stewardship and stimulate local stewardship conversion processes.

A parish might also wish to join the International Catholic Stewardship Council as a parish member. ICSC membership will pay great dividends through the materials and information the parish will receive throughout the year, as well as a reduced-price opportunity to attend the ICSC annual convention held in a different U.S. city each September.

Here's a final support strategy for parish stewardship committees: identify all nearby parishes that are engaged in a stewardship conversion process (even across diocesan lines). Invite their stewardship committees to form a regional coalition of parish committees as a stewardship conversion support group. Meet three or four times a year (or more often, if desirable), to share ideas and resources. Member parishes of this stewardship support-group could take turns hosting the gatherings. If one committee has the potential to be creative and productive, imagine what a committee of committees can do! See also Chapter 20 for a list of available resources to assist stewardship committees in their work.

CHAPTER 6

The Parish Newsletter

On any weekend, in any Catholic parish, it's abundantly evident that many registered parishioners are not in attendance at one of the scheduled Masses. In fact, across the U.S., fewer than half of those who identify themselves as Catholics regularly attend church services. Other parishioners, who *are* regular churchgoers, may be attending Mass in another church because of travel, convenience, and so on. These realities highlight the fallacy of using church bulletins and pulpit announcements as the principal means of communication within a parish. Furthermore, thanks to our flawed human nature, it's entirely likely that many parishioners will never read the bulletin that is pressed into their hands as they leave church. Still others may have already psychologically "checked out" at the end of Mass and are completely oblivious to the closing litany of announcements.

If a parish is firmly committed to the process of stewardship conversion, regular communication with *all* parishioners is absolutely essential. The challenge for parish leaders is to determine how best to place information about the parish in the hands, homes, and minds of every parishioner on a regular basis. Door-to-door visitations, while highly desirable, are unrealistic and impractical. Resurrecting the use of town criers would probably result in complaints about noise pollution. Telephoning every member would place the parish in the same category as the dreaded telemarketer. In short, there's only one viable option for total-parish communication: the United States Postal Service. And what must be mailed regularly to every parish household is a parish newsletter.

The parish newsletter is one of several essential tools in the stewardship conversion toolbox. Parishes that are serious about stewardship MUST publish a newsletter and mail a copy to every member's household. True to its name, a newsletter should be filled with news about parish activities, services, and programs, and names of as many parishioners as possible.

1. THE CASE FOR A NEWSLETTER

Professional marketing and communications experts tell us there are at least five good reasons for organizations to produce a newsletter:

A. Build Community and Loyalty

The more parishioners know about one another, the more they will feel attached to the parish family. In all but the smallest parishes, most parishioners are acquainted with only a few of their fellow parishioners. Particularly in the absence of multiple opportunities for personal contact, a newsletter helps to build a parish's community spirit.

B. Encourage Increased Participation

A parish newsletter is a time-and-talent building block, and a vital component of parish efforts to be welcoming and hospitable. A newsletter can be used to welcome, educate, promote, inform, and show gratitude. In addition to its obvious function as a parish bulletin board and roster of events, a newsletter gives parish staff members and volunteer leaders an outstanding medium for volunteer recruitment and retention.

C. Keep Lapsed or Former Members Within the Extended Parish Family

A newsletter provides a way to keep marginal and lapsed parishioners in touch with the parish. In other words, a parish newsletter is an excellent tool for evangelization. Unless inactive parishioners have moved away or otherwise officially discontinued their membership, they should continue to receive copies of the parish newsletter. A small, regular item in each issue inviting them back may be just the nudge they need to return to the fold. Or they may see a particular program, service, or activity that strikes their fancy which then becomes their avenue into more active participation.

D. Clarify, Enhance, or Improve the Parish's Image

A parish newsletter should be a "feel-good-piece." It should be treated as a public relations medium capable of displaying and energizing the spirit of the community. As it's being prepared for publication, its editors should be mindful of the power they have to positively influence the temperament of the parish.

SUGGESTION: send one issue of your newsletter each year to every parish in your diocese, and encourage other parishes with newsletters to do the same. This will be an invaluable resource for learning about what is happening in other parishes, and will give newsletter editors a great supply of creative data from which to draw helpful ideas about layout, writing style, types of items to include, and so on. Don't forget to add your diocesan newspaper to your newsletter mailing list.

E. Attract New Members

As an evangelization tool and component of a parish's welcoming and hospitality efforts, a parish newsletter is an important link with potential new members. Copies could be included in local welcome wagon materials; distributed through realtors; placed in public distribution sites in the parish neighborhood; sent or delivered personally to newly arrived Catholics, and so on.

2. WHAT MAKES A GOOD NEWSLETTER?

The answer to this question is limited only by the ingenuity of the parish staff and parishioners. A newsletter should be a work in progress that belongs to the entire parish. Every member should be invited to help improve its quality and content.

A. Essential Components

Listed below are the elements which should be included in every issue, followed by a suggested "value-added" list of items which could enhance a newsletter's readability.

- Attractive, appealing masthead
- Name/title (a catchy, clever name is a definite plus)

  TIP: Many parishes sponsor contests to name their newsletters. This tactic taps the entire parish's creative resources and generates broad interest in the newsletter from its inception.
- Date/issue (month, year, volume, number)
- Parish Mission Statement (if parish has one). This should be a permanent element included in the masthead.
- Names of staff members and how to reach them
- Parish address, phone and fax numbers, and web site and e-mail addresses, if available
- Mass schedule and opportunities to receive other sacraments, as needed
- Pastor's column
- Schedule of upcoming parish events and activities
- Reports from major parish committees and commissions
- Opportunities for volunteering along with instructions about how to get involved
- Instructions about how to submit items
- User-friendly layout and format: easily read typefaces; logical placement of items; appropriate headlines, and so on
- Name(s) of editor and/or editorial staff
- "Welcome newcomers" corner
- Information about Memorial and Honor Gifts (see Chapter 12)

B. Value-Added Elements

Here is a rundown of the value-added elements that might be present in a parish newsletter.

- Photographs (requires a high level of print quality)
- Graphics (many clip art sources are now available)
- Color (two-color printing is not expensive and adds a much more professional look to the final product. Avoid slick, expensive four-color processing.)
- Use recycled paper (with the official "recycled" logo)
- Birthdays/anniversaries
- Stewardship of treasure (status of budget) report

C. Other Questions About the Parish Newsletter

The following represent other questions that usually arise concerning the publishing of a parish newsletter:

- *How often should a newsletter be published?* Quarterly is acceptable, but monthly is preferred.
- *Who should be responsible for editing and publishing it?* Most parishes have staff members or parishioners gifted with the abilities to produce a quality newsletter. Ask staff members and trusted parish leaders to suggest possible editors. Do not issue a general call for volunteers. Ask to see a sample of each candidate's work. Because of the variety of skills necessary for a good newsletter (writing, layout, photographs, and so on), an editorial committee might be preferable to a single editor. A parish may be compelled to engage outside professional help to ensure a quality product.
- *What about the expense of printing and mailing?* A newsletter can add hundreds or even thousands of dollars to parish expenses, depending on the number printed, the frequency of publication, and the quality of the product. Parish leaders should consider ways to cover these expenses without adding a drain on parish resources. Here are a few options:

  — Offer advertising space to local businesses. NOTE: This strategy must be accompanied by competent legal advice and guidance from knowledgeable local postal officials. Three things to watch out for: (1) unrelated business income; (2) changing postal regulations; and (3) copyright laws.
  — Seek as much volunteer help and donated materials as possible.
  — Conduct an in-house annual special collection or special fundraiser.
  — Find "guardian angel" donors who are willing to underwrite the expenses.
  — Design the newsletter as a "self-mailer" which can be folded and mailed without a special envelope.

3. FINAL THOUGHTS

A parish newsletter's editorial staff should be absolutely committed to excellence. This means constantly seeking ways to improve its usefulness as a communications and public relations medium. In fact, the same commitment to excellence should apply to a parish's entire communication system. Even though a newsletter is a prime communications tool, it's not the only medium. Parish leaders should employ every appropriate means to communicate important information to their parishioners: the diocesan newspaper, other print media, radio, television, outdoor advertising, and direct mail.

CHAPTER 7

The Parish Directory

Nothing has more bearing on the success of stewardship conversion than the quality of parish communications. And one of the most useful time and talent communications media is a parish directory. (NOTE: "parish directory" in this context should not be confused with parish *pictorial* directories which several professional companies now produce for parishes. Note also that, in some parishes, the parish directory may have a different title such as parish resource book, parish time and talent brochure, parish guide, parish information handbook, and so on. While titles may vary, content and purpose are usually the same.)

1. THE BASIC ELEMENTS

Here are the basic elements that should be incorporated into a parish directory, followed by a list of supplemental items parish leaders may include.

- Statement of welcome from the pastor
- Parish name, address, and phone number (include fax number, web site address, and e-mail address, if available)
- Parish Mission Statement and identifying logo
- Table of contents
- Roster of parish staff members
- Mass schedules
- Times and places of other religious devotions
- Information about opportunities for the sacraments of reconciliation and anointing of the sick

- Brief history of the parish
- List of major parish commissions/boards including:
  (a) Names, addresses and phone numbers of officers and/or members
  (b) Description of activities and responsibilities
  (c) Time and place of meetings
- List of all other parish organizations including:
  (a) Description of their programs and services
  (b) Names and phone numbers of contact persons
  (c) Time and place of meetings, if applicable
- Emergency phone number for reaching a priest
- List and description or pictures of parish buildings
- Parish office hours
- Publication date of directory
- Invitation to become more involved in the parish along with a removable time and talent "sign-up" sheet
- Sacramental life instructions and policies (for example, R.C.I.A., marriage arrangements, funerals, baptisms, first Communion, confirmation, and so on)
- Schedule of major parish activities: parish social, annual awards night, ministry fair, thanksgiving banquet, parish picnic, and so on
- Available adult religious education programs
- Basic information about parish school and/or local Catholic high school, if applicable

2. VALUE-ADDED SUPPLEMENTAL ITEMS

The following gives some suggested value-added elements that may be part of a parish directory:

- Map showing parish boundaries
- Aerial view map or photo of parish campus with identifying indicators for each building and area
- List of diocesan services and how to access them
- Policies regarding use of parish facilities
- Various photos of people and events
- Parish membership roll
- Parish goals/objectives (from current long-range plan)

- Process for suggesting programs, services, or ministries not yet activated or available in the parish
- Organize all parish ministries and services in appropriate categories, such as social services, educational ministries, prayer/sacramental life, pastoral care, faith formation, administrative commissions, and so on
- Index of advertisers (if necessary)
- Statement of the parish's commitment to stewardship and how it affects the life of the parish
- Pertinent legal or parish policy statements (examples: bulletin/newsletter announcements, solicitations, use of parish mailing lists, and so on)
- Parish organizational chart
- Current parish budget and/or most recent annual financial report
- Blank pages for special notes

3. QUESTIONS AND SUGGESTIONS

The contents and style of a parish directory are limited only by the imagination of those who produce it. Here are a few issues and suggestions to consider as the directory is being prepared:

SUGGESTION: *Don't skimp just to save money.* The result may be a directory that is unattractive and unappealing to parishioners, newcomers, and prospective members.

QUESTION: *Should ads be included?* Beware! Selling advertising as a means of offsetting the expense of a directory could create an unrelated business income tax problem. See the section on "Catholic Fund-Raising and Taxes" in Chapter 11.

QUESTION: *Should a parish produce its own directory or use one of the parish directory publishing services?* No matter which option is selected, parish leaders must balance expense with the quality of the product. Remember: the directory is a premier public relations and time and talent tool for a parish. It should be a first-class publication that parishioners will use and share with pride.

SUGGESTION: *Rather than permanently bind the directories, distribute them in small, inexpensive three-ring binders so that pages can be inserted or replaced as needed.*

QUESTION: *Should parishes establish a presence on the World Wide Web?* Given today's rapidly changing technology and communications, plus the intense competition mainline churches are experiencing from many quarters, can parishes afford *not* to be on the Internet?

CHAPTER 8

Lay Witnesses

Lay witnessing is a powerful tool in the stewardship conversion toolbox. There are no more effective ways to inspire people to convert to a stewardship way of life than to hear fellow Christians recount their personal stewardship stories.

Several issues must be addressed when a parish chooses to add lay witnessing to its stewardship conversion process. The following sections present a brief overview of the key topics.

1. WHO SHOULD WITNESS?

Anecdotal evidence strongly suggests that the potency of lay witnessing is intensified if the witness is someone who is known and respected by the audience. Furthermore, stewardship witnessing by married couples tends to be more impressive and engaging than witnessing by an individual.

However, the answer to the question of who should witness stewardship in a parish must be discerned from the collective wisdom and style of the community. Each parish has a distinct communal personality which emanates from, and is nurtured by, a multitude of psychological, sociological, and theological factors. These factors must be taken into account as potential lay witnesses are considered. For example, who would best touch the hearts of the listeners? Who is regarded by most or all members to be good and faithful stewards? Should witness be given by resident parishioners or someone from outside the parish? (Many parishes deal with the latter question by using guest witnesses early in the parish's conversion process, but eventually replacing them with the parish's own members.)

2. TRAINING AND PREPARATION

If your diocesan stewardship office does not have a lay witness training program, it should at least be able to provide support and resource materials for selecting and preparing lay witnesses. Training should include *what* to say as well as *how* to say it. Group role-playing practice, with trainers' and fellow trainees' helpful feedback, is a must. Testing presentations on a few "guinea pig" parishioners is highly recommended.

Here are the basic elements which should be incorporated into all lay witness talks:

- Personal introduction
- Relationship to the parish
- Details of witnesses' personal stewardship journey and its current status (witnesses should not be too humble to mention successes or too proud to confess setbacks)
- What constitutes good stewardship? The U.S. bishops' definition is a good one. (See "Stewardship Conversion: A Process" on page xxiii of the Introduction.)
- How was the witness introduced to stewardship; who or what inspired and continues to inspire him or her
- How the witness's life is different since beginning the stewardship journey
- How does the witness decide what and how much time, talent, and treasure to give back to God
- An invitation to the audience to join in the journey

The content of the presentation is critical; witnesses should be instructed to "just be themselves" and talk openly about their efforts to be good stewards; sincerity is the key that unlocks hearts and minds. Parishioners will not expect rhetorical wizardry or bombastic oratory. Because people want to know that witnesses are real persons, humor, if appropriate, and sincere emotion are desirable. Live witness presentations could be reinforced by printing excerpts from the talks in subsequent issues of the parish newsletter.

3. PRACTICAL TIPS FOR LAY WITNESSES

Here are some practical tips for lay witnessing:

- Write out the talk and memorize it, but have it available for reference.
- Practice in church ahead of time with the sound system turned on.
- Be sure amplification system is in good working order just before the liturgy during which the talk is given; if a remote lavaliere (lapel) microphone is used, be sure it has a fresh battery.

4. ADDITIONAL CONSIDERATIONS

When is the best and/or proper time for lay witnessing during Mass? A response to this question raises several practical and liturgical issues. Laypersons are not allowed to give the homily during Mass; this is a privilege reserved only for someone who is ordained. On the other hand, giving a lay witness talk before or at the end of Mass will tend to compromise the effectiveness of the message. Decisions in these matters should be made by the parish's pastoral leaders in consultation with parishioners.

Since pastors come in all physical, attitudinal, and theological shapes and sizes, it's important that the pastor is completely aware of the nature of each lay-witness presentation and enthusiastically endorses it! As a simple matter of courtesy, the pastor should receive copies of lay-witness talks several days before they are given, along with a request for his input.

PART 2

STEWARDSHIP OF TREASURE

CHAPTER 9

Setting the Stage

The stewardship of treasure is mostly about money. And when the subject of money is broached within a religious context, a human version of the animal kingdom's fight or flight response is often triggered. Some people become contentious, while others emotionally flee the scene: they just don't want to hear it! One wag, upon hearing his pastor introduce a homily about the parish's need for more money, leaned toward his wife and quipped: "Uh, oh—here comes another 'Sermon on the Amount!'"

1. MONEY, MYTHS, AND MISUNDERSTANDINGS

There are several factors which contribute to the wide assortment of churchgoers' reactions to money. Here's a brief look at a few of them:

A. A Ruinous Misquotation

There's a provocative scriptural passage in 1 Timothy that addresses the money versus religion issue superbly. However, the common misquotation of one phrase from this passage may cause many Christians to respond negatively when money is mentioned in church. Here are excerpts from the passage; see if you can spot the misquotation. (NOTE: The writer of 1 Timothy is attempting to lay a few behavioral ground rules for an early Christian community whose members apparently had been engaging in conduct less than Christian. This condensed segment follows a series of instructions about proper behavior):

> Teach and urge these duties. Whoever teaches otherwise…is conceited, understanding nothing, and has a morbid craving for controversy….From these come envy, dissension, slander, base suspicions, and wrangling among those who are depraved in mind and bereft of the truth, imagining that godliness is a means of gain. Of course, there is great gain in godliness combined with contentment….But those who want to be rich fall into temptation and are trapped by many senseless and harmful desires that plunge people into ruin and destruction. For the love of money is a root of all kinds of evil, and in their eagerness to be rich some have wandered away from the faith and pierced themselves with many pains (1 Tim 6:2-10).

Did you notice the oft-misquoted phrase? The original text is "The *love of money* is a root of all kinds of evil," not "*money* is the root of all evil." The frequent incorrect quotation of this phrase may contribute to many Christians' irrational aversion for references to money within a church setting. Although money is sometimes used for evil purposes, it is not inherently evil. Money also spawns many corporal and spiritual works of mercy.

B. Where's the Theology of Money?

A second source of confusion about the relationship between money and religion is the fact that recent generations of Catholic religious leaders received theological education and spiritual formation which included little or no consideration of the stewardship of treasure. Consequently, many Church leaders are ill at ease when faced with the need to talk about money.

Many priests may have difficulty speaking of money because of the lifestyle they enjoy. Consider a priest—an *alter Christus*—living in a comfortable rectory, driving a new car, planning his next trip to Europe, occasionally eating in fine restaurants, with full health-insurance coverage and a generous retirement plan. He is expected to stand before a congregation which is struggling to pay mortgages, make car payments, feed, clothe, and educate children, and save for retirement, and ask them to put more money into their weekly envelopes! It's easy to understand his discomfort.

C. The Stewardship Attitude

A third reason why money and talk of money are often unwelcome in a church context is attitudinal: many Catholics seem to operate with a "give-to-need" frame of mind rather than from a stewardship-based "need-to-give" mode. One pastor recently characterized the give-to-need disposition as a "pay-the-bills mentality." Pay-the-bills (PTB) thinking works like this: when the collection basket is passed on Saturday or Sunday, a PTB parishioner tosses in a check or cash—loose or inside a contribution envelope—the amount of which is often determined by how he or she feels that day. PTB-ers give from a sense of duty or obligation. They're most likely to say: "Tell me how much you need, Father, and I'll decide how much I want to give."

Many PTB-ers are, from time to time, quite generous, but only when they are convinced of a specific need for their contribution and are asked to give. They rarely, if ever, give simply for the joy of giving, or out of gratitude for God's gifts. Tithing or proportional sacrificial giving is not even a consideration.

Give-to-need philanthropy has also been characterized as "giving to ourselves." When we share our resources only because we see the benefit to our parish, or because we like the pastor, or to please the person who asked us, we are not giving as Christian stewards. We are merely giving to serve our own purposes or to meet our own needs. Returning to God a portion of our treasure the steward's way means gratefully giving back some of God's property. It's giving for the sake of giving, without being asked, regardless of how our gifts will be used.

D. Is God the Source?

A possible fourth reason why talk of money often raises the ire of many churchgoers is because Christians tend to stumble over the phrase: "God is the source of everything." We explored the stewardship ramifications of this fundamental Christian tenet in Chapter 1. But we can never remind ourselves often enough that everything we are and have are gifts from God. We are but caretakers of God's property. Our eternal salvation depends on how we tend and use the possessions God loans us during our lifetimes.

Because of these skewed ideas and attitudes about money and stewardship, and perhaps for other reasons, the U.S. bishops found it necessary to call for a stewardship conversion in their 1992 pastoral, "Stewardship: A Disciple's Response." Here's what they had to say:

Following Jesus is the work of a lifetime. At every step forward, one is challenged to go further in accepting and loving God's will. Being a disciple is not just something else to do, alongside many other things suitable for Christians, it is a total way of life and requires continuing conversion.

2. WHO'S GIVING HOW MUCH TO WHOM AND WHY?

Each year the AAFRC (American Association of Fund-Raising Counsel) Trust for Philanthropy compiles and publishes a book entitled *Giving USA*. It's a fascinating collection of data about charitable giving in the United States. The 1999 issue (reporting 1998 figures) listed total contributions to nonprofit organizations as $174.52 billion, a 10.7 percent increase over the previous year. Here are a few highlights from the 1999 edition:

A. Where the Money Came From

- Individuals: $134.84 billion (77.3 percent of the total; increase over 1997: 9.7 percent)
- Foundations: $17.09 billion (9.8 percent of the total; increase over 1997: 22.9 percent)
- Bequests: $13.62 billion (7.8 percent of the total; increase over 1997: 6.2 percent)
- Corporations: $8.97 billion (5.1 percent of the total; increase over 1997: 9.3 percent)

B. Where the Money Went

- Religion: $76.06 billion (43.6 percent of total)
- Education: $24.56 billion (14.1 percent of total)
- Health: $16.89 billion (9.7 percent of total)
- Human Services: $16.08 billion (9.2 percent of total)
- Arts, Culture, and Humanities: $10.53 billion (6.0 percent of total)
- Gifts to Foundations: $16.94 billion (9.7 percent of total)
- Public/Society Benefit: $10.86 billion (6.2 percent of total)
- Environment/Wildlife: $5.25 billion (3.0 percent of total)
- International Affairs: $2.14 billion (1.2 percent of total)

It's evident from these numbers that individuals give an enormous amount of money to U.S. charities, particularly religious organizations.

C. Why People Give

Most fund-raisers know the standard list of the top five reasons why people give to charitable organizations. Of the top five reasons given by people for their charitable support, the most influential philanthropic motivator, by far, is belief in the institution and its purposes.

The remaining reasons, in descending order, are

- Belief that current needs are important
- Sense of loyalty, gratitude, affection
- Tax considerations
- Friendship and respect for those who ask

In other words, donor intent is altruistic at its core. Furthermore, a 1988 *Wall Street Journal* article reported a philanthropic phenomenon that continues to the present day: less affluent households give a greater percentage of their incomes to charities than do wealthier households. All charities, including religious organizations, must be mindful of these realities as they work to fulfill their missions and conduct fund-raising efforts.

D. What About Catholic Giving?

In 1987, Andrew Greeley and William McManus published *Catholic Contributions: Sociology and Policy* (Chicago: Thomas More Press), containing the results of their landmark research regarding U.S. Catholic giving. They reported that North American Catholics at that time were contributing 1.1 percent of their income to the church compared to 2.2 percent for Protestants. In a 1997 book entitled *Money Matters: Personal Giving in American Churches* (Louisville, Ken.: Westminster John Knox), Dean R. Hoge reported that Catholics gave only 1.4 percent of their income to the church whereas Protestants contributed 2.9 percent and the average non-Christian believer gave 3 percent.

In their book *Behind the Stained Glass Windows* (Grand Rapids, Mich.: Baker Books), researchers John and Sylvia Ronsvalle noted that most Christian giving can be characterized as "paying the bills." According to the Ronsvalles, the prevalent Christian attitude about stewardship of treasure is to give enough to cover parish or congregational expenses. This practice can explain some of the reported discrepancy between Catholic and Protestant giving. Catholic congregations are more efficiently organized with a much higher people-to-clergy ratio (that is, much larger parish rosters), which translates into lower per-household giving. But the Ronsvalles note that both Protestants and Catholics need to find an alternative view of stewardship rather than just paying the bills. They suggest that the question before church members is how to be faithful in the midst of affluence.

U. S. Catholics live in a social milieu that deifies accumulation and holds in highest esteem those who amass wealth. Living as a good Christian steward in the United States is, by almost any measure, countercultural. Yet an increasing number of Catholics are responding to Christ's call to discipleship and are choosing to embrace a stewardship way of life.

CHAPTER 10

Understanding the Concepts

We've already mentioned that living a stewardship way of life is unfamiliar territory for many of today's cradle Catholics. However, thanks to the U.S. bishops' pastoral letter on stewardship, the work of the International Catholic Stewardship Council, the dedicated efforts of diocesan stewardship and development offices, and the prophetic leadership of parishes and pastoral leaders throughout the U. S., the stewardship attitude that was a hallmark of early North American Catholic communities is making a comeback.

One of the measurable manifestations of a Catholic community's commitment to stewardship can be found in the way its members practice stewardship of treasure. We begin a closer look at the stewardship of treasure, and its complementary discipline, fund-raising, by clarifying a few basic concepts.

1. TITHING

Tithing is relatively easy to explain and understand, but not so easy to promote and practice. The classic scriptural description of tithing is "giving one's 'first fruits' back to God." The requirement for God's people to tithe has its roots in the Old Testament: "Set apart a tithe of all the yield of your seed that is brought in yearly from the field" (Deut 14:22); "The choicest of the first fruits of your ground you shall bring into the house of the LORD your God" (Ex 23:19); "All tithes from the land, whether the seed from the ground or the fruit from the tree, are the LORD's; they are holy to the LORD" (Lev 27:30).

The Christian tenet that a tithe is 10 percent of our "first fruits" comes from Genesis: "Of all that you give me I will surely give one tenth to you" (Gen 28:22). (See Appendix 1 for a comprehensive list of stewardship of treasure scriptural references.) The common interpretation of "first fruits," in today's vernacular, is 10 percent of gross earnings. For U.S. Christians, this means "before taxes" or, in IRS terminology, contributions based on adjusted gross income (AGI).

For several non-Catholic denominations, tithing is not an option or a goal, it's a requirement for membership which involves physically presenting a copy of one's annual tax records to church leaders! As already noted above, recent research on church giving clearly shows that tithing is no longer common among American Catholics. In fact, on average, Catholics give less than 2 percent of their annual incomes back to God compared to more than 2 percent for non-Catholics.

Returning a full tithe to God involves nearly heroic sacrifices for most Christians, given the nature of today's economy, social pressures, and lifestyle choices. Young families, in particular, struggle with mortgages, car payments, insurance premiums, student loans, taxes, raising children, and so on. The demise of the extended family as a reliable support system adds to the psychological and financial burdens felt by numerous families. Nevertheless, Catholics are slowly returning to the practice of tithing and are finding unexpected blessings and great comfort as a result.

Catholic stewardship and development professionals suggest this formula for the distribution of a 10 percent tithe: 5 percent is given to the parish, 4 percent goes to other charities, and 1 percent is contributed to the diocese. When a parish engages in a capital campaign, some or all of the "4 percent goes to other charities" portion can be used by parishioners to fulfill a campaign pledge. Furthermore, parishioners who are so inclined should not feel constrained to limit themselves to a traditional 10 percent tithe.

What percentage of income an individual or family gives back to God is determined by many variables. But the fundamental charitable motivation for good stewards is always the same: gratitude for the many blessings God has showered on them. For most Christians, choosing to tithe is simply a matter of rearranging priorities. For example, a family may choose to keep a family car for eight years instead of four, or they may purchase an older home with an $800 monthly mortgage payment instead of a new home with a $1,400 monthly payment, or they may shop at Wal-Mart instead of Lord & Taylor and Abercrombie & Fitch, and so on. Underlying every financial decision is the good steward's confidence that God will not be outdone in generosity.

2. PROPORTIONAL GIVING

Proportional giving, like tithing, requires a conscious, calculated decision to return to God a predetermined percentage of one's annual income. Unlike tithing, however, it's typically a "floating percentage"—usually less than 10 percent—based on various factors which an individual, couple, or family takes into consideration. Within a stewardship of treasure context, proportional giving is a common method of gradually moving toward a full tithe. A common proportional giving scenario begins with a parishioner's calculation of his or her current percent-of-income charitable giving. The next step is a decision to increase the percentage by 1 or 2 percent each year until the full 10 percent tithe has been reached.

3. WHAT'S THE PAYOFF?

A few of the "electronic evangelists" seem to imply that sending them a charitable contribution will ensure a great windfall in the donor's life. Such a message is antithetical to the stewardship way of life. Good stewards do not "give to get"; they are simply returning a portion of God's own possessions!

But there is, in fact, a magnificent payoff for those who practice good stewardship of treasure. One veteran Christian steward described it this way: "Ever since I accepted Christ's stewardship mandate, I've become incredibly sensitized to the many gifts and blessings God pours over me and my family every day—so many things I used to take for granted. It's overwhelming! I can't begin to thank God enough. Even giving 10 percent back seems puny compared to what God has given me!"

4. THE STEWARDSHIP SOLUTION REVISITED

In the introduction to this book, we mentioned the "stewardship solution": the quantum leap of faith parishes and individual Christians make in adopting total stewardship. The treasure portion of the stewardship solution can exert a profound and measurable impact on the financial health of a parish. (See item number five of the "Ten Characteristics of a Total-Stewardship

Parish" in Appendix 7.) Here is an example of that potential impact on a typical parish:

Saint Facetious Parish is located in a middle-class urban-suburban neighborhood. The average annual household income is $51,000. There are about 1,800 parishioners (600 households). Last year's offertory collections totaled $530,000 or about $883 per household ($17 per week). In other words, on average, Saint Facetious parishioners currently give less than 2 percent of their annual household incomes to the parish.

If Saint Facetious parishioners would adopt the practice of proportional giving and increase their average giving to *3 percent of household income* (an additional $9.00 per household per week, on average), total annual offertory collections would increase by $265,200, or $5,100 per week. If parishioner giving would increase to *4 percent of income* per household (an average total of $34.00 per week per household), weekly collections would increase by $10,200 for a whopping total of $1,060,800 annually!

In other words, a modest 1 or 2 percent annual increase in Saint Facetious parishioners' stewardship of treasure would ensure the parish's financial future forever! Extra fund-raisers could continue, but the revenue they generate would no longer be needed for operating expenses; it could be used to complete deferred maintenance, build a parish endowment, provide assistance to less fortunate parishes, and so on. With its financial worries put aside, the parish could focus its entire energy and resources on serving God's people and building God's kingdom!

CHAPTER 11

Catholic Fund-Raising And the Law

The Roman Catholic Church enjoys a distinct legal status in the United States. Its entities are educational, charitable, and religious institutions according to section 501(c)(3) of the Internal Revenue Code. It operates as a confederation of unique and loosely organized civil-type corporations which are also governed by the legal system of the Roman Catholic Church as delineated in its Code of Canon Law. This confluence of civil and ecclesiastical jurisdictions can create tensions which cause legal and financial professionals from both camps to scratch their heads.

One of the greatest sources of personal consternation for many Catholics is faulty information given by their legal and financial advisors who don't understand the subtle nuances created by the juxtaposition of two legal systems. Ignorance of these nuances can profoundly affect taxation, legal, and financial advice given to Catholic clients, particularly those with significant charitable intentions.

In this section, we will review many of the pivotal legal and financial issues which affect Catholic charitable giving, estate planning, and fund-raising. Because Catholic fund-raising includes many diverse activities (see Chapter 12), discussion of the items in this chapter will be broad-based. Please note that much of the information you will find here is subject to frequent change and therefore should serve only as a foundation for further investigation and study. The reader should seek competent professional help to obtain the most reliable and up-to-date information regarding the topics outlined below.

1. CIVIL LAW AND CANON LAW: AN OVERVIEW

Before we begin our discussion, it will be helpful to keep a few definitions in mind.

- *Civil Law:* the public laws of the United States and of its respective individual states.
- *Canon Law:* the legal system of the Catholic Church, governing all its internal affairs including the administration of temporal goods.
- *Diocese:* "A diocese is a portion of the people of God which is entrusted for pastoral care to a bishop with the cooperation of the presbyterate [that is, the priests of the diocese] so that, adhering to its pastor [that is, the bishop] and gathered by him in the Holy Spirit through the gospel and Eucharist, it constitutes a particular church in which the one, holy, catholic and apostolic Church of Christ is truly present and operative" (Canon 369).
- *Parish:* "A parish is a definite community of the Christian faithful established on a stable basis within a particular church; the pastoral care of the parish is entrusted to a pastor as its own shepherd under the authority of the diocesan bishop" (Canon 515, § 1).

A. Ownership of Church Property

When the question of who owns Catholic church property is raised, the answer hinges not only on the definitions of diocese and parish given above, the canonical responsibilities of bishops and pastors, and the fundamental canon law concepts of "dominium" and "juridic person," but also must take into consideration any pertinent civil laws. *Dominium* is a term from Roman law that signifies absolute, undivided ownership of property. Dominium includes the right to possess and use property, the right to income generated by the property, and the right to manage and convey property. A "juridic person" signifies a group of persons or things which is the subject of canonical rights and obligations transcending the physical persons which make them up, and which is ordered toward a purpose congruent with the mission of the Church; for example, a diocese, parish, or religious order. (NOTE: This concept is similar to a "corporation" in civil law.)

So who actually owns Catholic church property? Following the canonical concepts outlined on the previous page, along with several canons which delineate the duties, rights, and responsibilities of bishops and pastors, church property belongs to the juridic person who has dominium. A common parish/diocesan ownership structure in the United States entails each entity within a diocese with a separately incorporated civil legal status. For variations of this type of structure, see page 109 of *The Parish in Catholic Tradition* by James Coridon (Mahwah, N.J.: Paulist Press, 1997). In other words, the diocese, as a juridic person, owns diocesan properties and assets; the parish, as a juridic person (that is, the community of the faithful along with its pastor), owns parish properties and assets.

According to canon law, the bishop or pastor is responsible for the property which he administers in the name of the juridic person. The bishop, as administrator of the diocese, "signs off" on all official diocesan business, just as the pastor or any official substitute for the pastor acts in the name of the parish regarding official parish business. Local state laws should be consulted regarding who is responsible for the civil law administration of church property.

B. Diocese As "Corporation Sole"

Some U.S. dioceses have structured their civil legal entity as a "corporation sole." Under this rubric, all property and assets belong to the juridic person that is the diocese. In a manner similar to that of a civil corporation, the bishop, as administrator of the diocese and head of the corporation sole, holds title to all property of the diocese. This civil structure allows the church to retain its own canonical form, with ownership being attributed to the proper juridical person. This type of unified diocesan property-holding mechanism also has a few legal variations. James Coridon's *The Parish in Catholic Tradition* gives further details about a "corporation sole" and its variants.

C. When Parishes Begin and End

Clergy shortages and continuously shifting populations create an endless demographic ripple effect which impacts the real estate and personnel needs of every diocese. Over time, neighborhoods spring up, thrive, and die—and Catholic parishes and schools with them. Many U.S. dioceses today are being forced to confront painful decisions regarding the future of parishes in changing neighborhoods. Closing parishes with many years of history is a tragic reality of our highly mobile society.

The process of establishing a new parish—or discontinuing an existing one—is clearly spelled out in canon law. The bishop is the only person who can set up, close, or notably alter a parish—but not before consulting with his presbyteral (priests') council. There may also be civil legal overtones for such procedures, depending on how a diocese is legally structured.

D. Disposition of Church Property

Whether organized as separate individual corporations of a diocese and each of its parishes, or as a corporation sole, no bishop or pastor may dispose of church goods any way he wants to. Church law places many restrictions on those who administer church possessions—the canonical equivalent of a system of checks and balances which regulates the ownership of church property. Failure to handle church assets in an appropriate manner could lead to the imposition of church penalties. Furthermore, no clear-thinking bishop or pastor, as Christ's representative on earth, would presume to destroy the trust the faithful freely place in them by capriciously and unilaterally attempting to make decisions about the disposition of church belongings.

In the United States, for example, any diocesan or parish financial transaction involving extraordinary (that is, beyond day-to-day) administration of church property or assets valued at $3,000,000 or more must be reviewed and formally approved by the Holy See in Rome. Diocesan and parish extraordinary transactions between $500,000 and $3,000,000 require the consent of the diocesan finance council and diocesan college of consultors—not just their consultation, but their consent! (Members of diocesan finance councils and colleges of consultors are appointed by the bishop as his advisors in financial and certain other diocesan matters. Finance council members may be clergy or laypersons; college of consultors members are priests only.)

Parish extraordinary transactions between $500,000 and $3,000,000 also require the consent of the pastor, parish financial council and, in many dioceses, the parish pastoral council. (Canon law requires each parish to have a finance council to advise the pastor in financial matters.) The bishop may also set limits for financial actions which could not be exceeded on the parish level without his written permission.

Why is it necessary to raise and discuss these issues? Because diocesan fund-raisers are frequently queried by donors who want to know how "safe" are the contributions they make to their parishes or dioceses. Here are a few commonly asked questions: "Who's going to stop my pastor or any future pastor from doing anything he wants with my bequest for church maintenance?" "What if the bishop decides he wants to use the money I gave to the retired clergy fund to pay for his next vacation?" "Suppose some large corporation offers 'the diocese' a boatload of money to buy our Catholic high school—would the bishop be able to sell it if he liked the offer?" In the wake of recent fund-raising scandals involving high-profile church officials, such concerns are not misguided!

2. CATHOLIC FUND-RAISING AND TAXES

Each year the United States Catholic Conference receives a letter from the appropriate District Director of the Internal Revenue Service regarding a 1946 IRS ruling. Here's the important first paragraph of this annual letter:

> In a ruling dated March 25, 1946, we [that is, the Internal Revenue Service] held that the agencies and instrumentalities and all educational, charitable and religious institutions operated, supervised or controlled by or in connection with the Roman Catholic Church in the United States, its territories or possessions appearing in the Official Catholic Directory for 1946, are entitled to exemption from federal income tax under the provisions of section 101(6) of the Internal Revenue Code of 1939, which corresponds to section 501(c)(3) of the 1986 Code. This ruling has been updated annually to cover the activities added to or deleted from the Directory.

In other words, any organization or institution whose name appears in each year's edition of *The Official Catholic Directory*, published by P. J. Kenedy & Sons, is tax-exempt, provided that it continues to comply with the requirements outlined in the annual letter; any charitable contributions made to it are, therefore, tax deductible to the extent provided in the Internal Revenue Code. Copies of the current annual IRS letter ruling should be readily available in every Catholic parish, school, or organization which receives charitable contributions. In an imperfect world, stewardship of treasure decisions may be tax driven; some donors are much more willing to give if a tax deduction is available. Consequently, Catholic organizations should maintain vigilance in ensuring that deductions are available.

A. Tuition, Stewardship, and the IRS

From time to time, it's wise for parish leaders to revisit the issue of the tax deductibility of Catholic school tuition. This is especially true for parishes which are, in some manner, fiscally responsible for the operation of a local or regional Catholic elementary or high school, and which are seriously promoting a total stewardship way of life among their parishioners.

Regardless of one's personal feelings or opinions about the relative fairness of this issue, the IRS definitively stated its position in Revised Rule 83-104 in 1983 and has subsequently reinforced it with several related rulings and court cases. Every Catholic parish and school should have a copy of these documents or at least a synopsis of them, such as the excellent paper by Wayne Martin LeNell entitled "Charitable Contribution or Tuition?" (Durand, Ill.: The Durand Corporation, no date).

The fundamental rule is quite simple: taxpayers may deduct charitable contributions made to qualified organizations, but they may not deduct tuition payments. Confusion—and often illegal activity—arises when parish leaders or Catholic school officials attempt to circumvent the law through semantics; "tuition" becomes "suggested contribution" or "required support." The celebrated, quasi-legal "duck law" applies here: if it walks like a duck and quacks like a duck, it's a duck. The IRS has consistently held that tuition by any name is still tuition and is not tax deductible.

There is, however, one very narrow scenario by which contributions to a parish which, at least in part, support a Catholic school, are, indeed, tax deductible. This model, designed by the IRS and clearly spelled out in Revised Rule 83-104, requires that parishioners whose children attend a parish school be treated no differently from all other parishioners regarding their financial contributions to the parish. In this scenario, a parish's Catholic school is an integral component of the parish's total mission and array of services and programs. All parishioners are encouraged to contribute as generously as they can—usually by tithing or proportional giving—to support all of the parish's activities. Parents of school children are not singled out for special treatment regarding their contributions to the parish. All parish families are eligible to send their children to the parish school regardless of their level of parish support. The school is, in effect, free, or at least tuition-free, for all parishioners. (Parents who are not members of the parish may, however, be required to pay tuition; their tuition payments are not tax deductible.)

What does all of this mean in the real world? At this writing, we are unaware of any instance when someone has "blown the whistle" on a diocese or large group of parishes where school families have improperly deducted tuition payments made as contributions to a parish. Could it happen that someone would expose such a practice to the IRS? Yes. Is it likely to happen? Probably not. However, we should remember that the IRS offers a "finder's fee" of 10 percent of the taxes recovered to anyone who alerts the Service about lost revenue caused by someone not playing by the rules. A single disgruntled parishioner or vindictive person with an anti-Catholic bias could create serious problems for some Catholic school families.

B. Unrelated Business Income Taxes

In 1950, the U.S. Congress inserted into the Internal Revenue Code a tax on the income from any unrelated trade or business conducted by a tax-exempt organization. The purpose for this action was twofold: (1) to counteract unfair competition by nonprofit organizations, which pay no taxes, with businesses which must pay taxes; and (2) to increase revenues for the U.S. Treasury. This legislation was prompted by a growing number of nonprofit organizations engaging in a fund-raising strategy known as "shared cost-based market piggybacking" (SCMP). This strategy refers to a nonprofit organization establishing a for-profit business activity, in a market which is at least marginally related to the organization's primary mission, as a means of subsidizing that organization's deficit-producing mission. (See the section on "piggybacking" in Chapter 16: "Nontraditional Fund-Raising Sampler.)

Since the early 1980s, the U.S. Small Business Administration, on behalf of many of the companies it serves, has complained vociferously about the burgeoning use of piggybacking by nonprofit organizations to fund their operations. Because of these complaints, the Internal Revenue Service has intensified its scrutiny of unrelated business activity among nonprofit organizations.

Diocesan and pastoral officials must be very careful about the methods they select to generate revenue. Particularly risky practices include paid advertising in diocesan newspapers, parish bulletins, and church newsletters, and rental of church buildings when the activities for which the buildings are rented have no apparent relationship to the religious or educational mission of the church (for example, diocesan retreat or educational facilities which are "rented out" to for-profit businesses for training programs, corporate retreats, recreation, and so on).

An unrelated business income tax case which is currently working its way through the legal system, and which has gained notoriety in recent years, is the Sierra Club's affinity credit card. The IRS contends that income generated from such credit cards is unrelated business income since it involves selling a product, which is the credit card. The Sierra Club, along with hundreds of other charitable and educational institutions which sponsor affinity card programs, contends that the income is royalty, not unrelated business income, and is therefore not taxable. At this writing, lower courts have decided in favor of the Sierra Club, but the final chapter has yet to be written on this matter.

C. Nonprofit Political Activity

Another issue which could create serious tax exemption difficulties for church entities is the Internal Revenue Service prohibition against certain types of political activities by nonprofit institutions. The IRS position is quite clear: if a nonprofit organization engages in activity that can be construed as partisan or issue-oriented political campaigning, that organization's nonprofit status will be revoked. As each election season approaches, the Office of the General Counsel for the United States Catholic Conference usually issues a memo detailing current electioneering dos and don'ts for Catholic entities. Educating both candidates and voters about specific issues and the church's stand on those issues is certainly allowed. What is disallowed are endorsements or statements of opposition for specific candidates, providing targeted financial support or access to mailing lists, and sponsorship of Political Action Committees.

Church leaders are well-advised to stay abreast of the latest IRS pronouncements about acceptable and unacceptable activities during political campaign periods. There is often a fine line between educating voters and promoting candidates or issues. Crossing that line could reap highly undesirable consequences for a parish or diocese.

3. ETHICAL AND MORAL ISSUES

Several ethical and moral issues in connection with Catholic fund-raising should be brought forward. These pertain to the issues of undue influence and gambling.

A. *Undue Influence*

Not long ago, there was an extraordinary news story about a university professor and his wife, Donald and Mildred Othmer, who, before their deaths, had amassed a combined estate of $750 million. Their incredible wealth was the result of frugal living coupled with the fact that they had invested their savings over a period of many years with stock market guru Warren Buffett. Most of the estate was bequeathed to charities and institutions. A small portion went to family members. The news story concluded with this sentence: "But already, a niece of Mrs. Othmer, who is to receive about $2 million, has said her family *deserves* more of the money."

Wherever there are prospective donors for a parish or school, particularly donors with sizable assets, there are often prospective heirs—many with only remote relationships to the donors—who somehow believe they have a *right* to a portion of the assets. And they're eager to claim their share! Pastors, bishops, and other religious leaders must attentively and knowledgeably negotiate a potential legal mine field referred to as "undue influence," particularly when cultivating elderly parishioners with accumulated wealth.

In U.S. jurisprudence, undue influence is defined as "any improper or wrongful constraint, machination, or urgency of persuasion whereby the will of a person is overpowered and he is induced to do or forbear an act which he would not do or would do if left to act freely" (see the fuller definition in Black's Law Dictionary). In other words, undue influence deprives the person who is influenced of his or her freedom to act or choose by replacing his or her will with the will of another.

There are several circumstances which impact legal proceedings regarding undue influence. Some of these are

- Confidential relationship between the donor and someone who benefits from the donor's gift
- Active solicitation, which involves the gift recipient promising something to the donor in return for the gift
- The donor's fanaticism toward a particular beneficiary
- The donor's predisposition to make gifts to the gift recipient
- Failure to provide for the donor's family (when a gift causes the donor or his or her family to become impoverished)

The confidential relationship situation is the basis for a large percentage of undue influence claims and is often related to the other circumstances mentioned previously. In several cases, the courts have held that undue influence is presumed between a spiritual advisor and a parishioner, just as it is presumed in attorney-client, parent-child, and physician-patient relationships. In other words, parish pastoral leaders must be especially cautious when interacting with donors who might be perceived as susceptible to undue influence.

Some of the factors which attorneys may claim indicate a donor's susceptibility to undue influence include the donor's mental and physical condition, whether the donor relied on the spiritual advisor for personal and financial advice, past history of giving to the organization, and so on. Ordinarily, for example, a bequest made through a properly drawn will, professionally prepared, is a safe way to make a charitable gift to an organization. However, a will can be contested, and its provisions invalidated, when undue influence is proven.

In other words, prospective charitable-gift beneficiaries of a donor's philanthropy should steer clear of any activity which could be interpreted as inordinately influencing the donor to include the beneficiaries in his or her lifetime giving or estate plan. Remember, a charitable beneficiary needs only to be *accused* of undue influence. The result could be a financially catastrophic court battle which might consume the entire charitable gift!

B. Gambling With Gambling

Within a religious context, gambling as a fund-raising strategy carries inordinately negative baggage. All gambling activities—even the hallowed Catholic staple, bingo—raise moral implications and elicit a public perception that is skewed by gambling's well-known association with undesirable elements within U.S. society. Because of the large sums of money that change hands each year through gambling, it's inevitable that less-than-honorable people are attracted to gambling like hungry mosquitoes to bare human skin.

Furthermore, as an ever-expanding number of states enter the gambling business through state lotteries, or as states extend the limits of what constitutes legal gambling within their jurisdictions, these same states tend to enact increasingly stringent legislation regulating nonprofit gambling activities which constitute direct competition for state-sponsored gambling.

It's increasingly risky and complicated for Catholic parishes, schools and other organizations to conduct their gambling "business as usual." More than one Catholic organization has been publicly embarrassed by its members who have failed to comply with state and local gaming laws. And we already know that local and national news media are more than happy to ferret out Church officials who bend or break the law. Furthermore, jokes about Catholic bingo, the "eighth sacrament," not only border on the mean-spirited but also humiliate and thwart Church leaders who are intent on developing a true spirit of stewardship among U.S. Catholics.

Before adding—or continuing—gambling activities as fund-raisers, parish leaders should prayerfully weigh their benefits and liabilities. Because of today's legally complicated and litigious society, it's highly advisable to engage competent legal counsel to carefully research all local and state gambling regulations.

We offer one final observation in this matter: in a total-stewardship parish, gambling to raise money is not only antithetical to the stewardship way of life, it is, in fact, unnecessary.

4. MONEY AND THE CATHOLIC CHURCH

Two money-related issues may need explanation, especially to lay members of the Church: the diocesan bank and Mass stipends and stole fees.

A. The Diocesan Bank (Deposit and Loan Funds)

Parish and diocesan officials often hear comments like these from laypersons: "I want to put something in my will for my parish, but I don't want the bishop to get his hands on my money"; "Someone told me that whenever a parish gets a big gift from someone, the diocese gets half the money"; "I heard that the bishop owns everything in the diocese, so he can take all of our parish's money anytime he wants it."

These and similar comments are fueled by an unfortunate and somewhat bewildering mistrust and animosity many laypeople and some priests harbor toward "the diocese." Attempting to understand and explain the source of these irrational feelings toward a diocesan central administration would occupy an army of psychologists and social scientists well into this new millennium. We suspect, however, that much of this enduring lack of trust can be traced to bad information. When parish leaders and laypeople, out of malice or ignorance, transmit false rumors and misinformation about diocesan procedures and policies, they knowingly or unknowingly perpetuate a destructive adversarial climate within a diocese.

One example of how bad information can damage the relationship between diocesan leadership and parish membership often surfaces when a diocese administers a service for parishes commonly known as a "deposit and loan fund." Diocesan deposit and loan funds are marvelous internal banking mechanisms designed to provide much-needed financial assistance for parishes, schools, and other diocesan entities. They work like this: parishes with excess funds (beyond ordinary operational needs) are required to deposit these funds in the diocesan treasury. The parishes, in turn, receive a reasonable rate of interest.

Parish money placed in a deposit and loan fund is available to be loaned to other parishes, schools, or diocesan organizations, usually for major capital improvement projects. When funds are borrowed from a deposit and loan fund, the borrowing entity pays a modest rate of interest that is typically well below local commercial loan rates.

Deposit and loan funds are outstanding cooperative ventures between a diocese and its parishes which benefit all participants. (NOTE: Deposit and loan fund administrators should regularly review state banking laws to be sure such practices are legal.) Yet, this laudable arrangement is often erroneously depicted as "the diocese taking our parish money." Ironically, it's often the same people who complain loudest about being "forced" to turn over excess funds to the diocese, who are the quickest to request money from the fund for a new church, to renovate a school, or to make other capital improvements!

B. Mass Stipends and Stole Fees

Laypeople are often confused and somewhat dismayed by the Catholic practice of priests accepting money for Masses and other ministerial services. They ask: "Is it not part of a priest's job to say Mass, dispense sacraments such as baptism and matrimony, and officiate at funerals? Aren't priests already paid to do these things?" As the U.S. Catholic laity becomes more involved and conversant with the operation of their parishes, such questions will become increasingly common.

Church law is unequivocally explicit about the subjects of Mass offerings (also called "stipends") and offerings that are given for sacraments and parish functions (called "stole fees").

In regard to Mass offerings, canon law says the following: "It is lawful for any priest who celebrates or concelebrates Mass to receive an offering to apply the Mass according to a definite intention" (Canon 945, § 1). John M. Huels in his *The Pastoral Companion* (Quincy, Ill.: Franciscan Press, 1995, page 110) says: "There can be no more than one offering conjoined with an intention accepted by each priest for a single Mass." Canon 951, section 1 further says that a priest who presides at more than one Mass on the same day may apply each one for an intention for which an offering is given; that on Christmas, a priest may keep offerings for three Masses celebrated; and that on all other days he may keep only one offering, and give the others to purposes prescribed by the ordinary [the bishop].

The amount of these offerings is set either by the bishops within a province or by local diocesan custom. No one is allowed to accept more Mass offerings to be applied by himself than he is able to satisfy within a year (Canon 953). When a priest or parish receives more stipends than can be used, they are typically turned over to priests in religious orders or in foreign missions. In other words, when Catholic clients ask their attorneys to include hundreds or even thousands of dollars for "Masses" in their wills, many if not all of the Masses will probably be said by priests in some distant land. Furthermore, according to Roman Catholic theology, when a Mass is "said" for someone, the amount of grace or spiritual benefit that person receives is as great from one Mass as it is from one thousand Masses. Therefore, Catholics might be encouraged to rethink the value of bequeathing a large sum of money for Masses. An appropriate charitable endowment gift for a parish or Catholic school might be a more desirable way of extending a donor's legacy.

In terms of stole fees, Canon 531 states that all stole fees (that is, offerings given by the faithful for certain parochial functions such as baptisms, weddings, funerals, and so on) and other voluntary offerings given to pastors, other priests, deacons, and lay ministers, are to be turned over to a parish fund to be used for the purpose specified by the bishop. Further, Huels in his *The Pastoral Companion* (page 331) says that any voluntary offering given over and above the established amount can be kept by the minister only if it is clear that this was the donor's intention. If there is any doubt about the donor's intention, the offering goes entirely to the parish fund.

5. ADVICE FOR ADVISORS

In this chapter, we have attempted to highlight several common areas of legal and financial confusion regarding the operation of the Catholic Church. Financial and legal advisors should never assume that their Catholic clients are aware of, or comprehend, the topics outlined in this chapter. Attorneys, accountants, stockbrokers, financial planners, and insurance agents have a professional responsibility to provide all of their clients, including Catholics, with accurate legal and financial counsel.

We strongly recommend that financial and legal advisors seek competent counsel themselves from someone well-versed in the intricacies of Catholic law and customs before recommending courses of action for their Catholic clients.

CHAPTER 12

The Fund-Raising Menu

This chapter addresses fund-raising options that may be used by parishes. The options range from capital campaigns to memorial gifts to government grants.

1. THE ANNUAL FUND

Are you solicited each year for a United Way pledge? Do you receive at least one mailing or phone call from an alma mater every year asking for a contribution? As a member of a Catholic parish, are you approached annually for a donation to a diocesan appeal? If any or all of the above applies to you, you are already familiar with the annual fund.

An annual fund is exactly what its name implies: a once-a-year effort by a charitable organization to raise money from its members, donors, or constituents. Your mailbox knows a lot about annual funds. If you've ever responded to a direct-mail request for a donation, your name is indelibly etched on that charity's list of donors and you will probably be solicited for annual gifts. (As one television evangelist observed: "The United States Postal Service is my collection plate!")

Most U.S. Catholic dioceses now conduct annual fund drives with names like "Annual Diocesan Appeal," "Bishop's Stewardship Appeal," "Diocesan Development Fund," "Archbishop's Annual Catholic Appeal," and so on. In addition, Catholics are all too familiar with several national special collections conducted in their parishes each year: Catholic Relief Services, Campaign for Human Development, Mission Sunday, and Peter's Pence, to name just a few. These, too, are annual funds.

The annual fund strategy has a direct relationship to stewardship of treasure. In our discussion of tithing in Chapter 10, we outlined the commonly recommended distribution for a Christian's traditional 10 percent tithe: 5 percent to the parish, 4 percent for other charitable purposes, and 1 percent to the diocese. Charities which conduct annual fund drives, other than diocesan appeals, are vying for a share of the "4 percent for other charitable purposes."

What you need to know about annual funds: Annual funds differ from capital campaigns in several ways. An annual fund is usually designed to raise yearly operating funds for an organization. A capital campaign is a "sometime thing" which occasionally becomes necessary because of specific needs that exceed ordinary operating expenses.

Annual fund pledges are made for the duration of the year for which they are solicited. Contributions to capital campaigns are usually made in the form of multiyear pledges.

Annual funds target donors or donor prospects who comprise an organization's membership roster. Diocesan annual funds, for example, solicit all registered Catholic households within a diocese. Annual fund campaigns for schools primarily target alumni and parents of current or former students. (If you are a Catholic school graduate or the parent of a Catholic school student, you are most likely solicited annually by your alma mater or by the school your child attends since many Catholic schools now have professionally staffed development offices.)

Donor prospects for capital campaigns, on the other hand, include any person or company which has a relationship, however remote, with the school or organization.

Professional fund-raisers recommend face-to-face solicitations for both annual funds and capital campaigns—and rightly so. Personal solicitations inevitably generate the best results. But the repetitive nature of the annual fund often works against this professional recommendation. Here's a familiar scenario: a professional fund-raising company is hired to establish a diocesan annual fund drive. Initially there's a great flurry of volunteer organization, training, and motivation. Door-to-door personal solicitations are the primary modus operandi. But the consultants eventually collect their fees and depart, leaving the fund drive in the hands of capable, yet often overwhelmed, development officers. In most settings, it's impossible to sustain the high level of local leadership support, volunteer organization, training, and enthusiastic motivation, year after year, for door-to-door canvassing.

Consequently, many diocesan annual funds, begun with professional direction and heavily dependent on household visitations, eventually evolve into "in-pew," direct mail, and phonathon events.

Most parishes do not utilize the annual fund strategy for their own purposes since they typically rely on weekly offertory collections to fund their operations. For a total-stewardship parish, an annual fund drive would be superfluous.

What you need to have to conduct an annual fund: The following elements are necessary concomitants to successful annual fund drives.

- *Accurate donor records.* There are dozens of excellent computer software packages on the market which are designed specifically for fund-raising and development needs. Two periodicals, *Contributions* and *Fund-Raising Management* publish annual buyers' guides for fund-raising software.
- *Ability to process pledges.* This includes a system to track pledge payments and generate periodic pledge payment reminders. The system should also be able to generate personalized "thank yous" for each gift which should be mailed within a day or two after gifts are received.
- *Compelling direct mail pieces.* If you're considering using direct mail as an element of an annual fund campaign, you must first consider the level of competition in the direct mail industry. If your mail pieces look like junk mail, they will be treated accordingly!
- *Cadre of zealous, well-trained, highly motivated phonathon volunteers (most annual funds have a phonathon component).* Phonathon volunteers take enormous risks when they face the great unknown of each phone call. Good prephonathon training, and strong during-phonathon support are vital elements for a successful telephone fund-raising event. There are several competent professional telemarketing companies which will conduct the phonathon component of an annual fund drive. However, caveat emptor!
- *Potent, year-round communications/public relations program.* It can't be said too often: good communications are critical for fund-raising and the stewardship conversion process. Keeping donors abreast of an organization's activities and status helps to ensure the success of its annual fund.

- *User-friendly materials.* Remember that an annual fund is a *fund-raising* strategy. Contributing should be as simple as possible. Reply devices should be easy to fill out, and postage-paid return envelopes are strongly recommended.
- *Ability to personalize.* Most annual funds rely at least in part on direct mail. Any items mailed to donor prospects—particularly letters—must be accurately personalized.
- *Realistic budget.* Professional fund-raisers know that it costs money to raise money. Although it's possible to create annual fund campaigns which are excessively expensive, it's also possible to critically wound a campaign by skimping on materials and supplies.
- *Adequate training and support for volunteers.* When an annual fund drive includes a volunteer component, campaign leaders must remember that volunteers are indeed volunteers; they're not professional fund-raisers. They will require sufficient training and they will need to know that competent support is available for them should they need it.

What you need to do to conduct an annual fund drive: Here is a list of action steps to be taken in the conduct of an annual fund drive:

- Meticulously organize every campaign detail
- Set a realistic campaign schedule, and stick to it
- Develop attractive—but not too expensive looking—user-friendly campaign materials; test the materials on several trusted donors before making final decisions
- Personalize and "live-stamp" everything that will be sent through the mail
- Train and support volunteer solicitors
- Promote the campaign through every possible communications medium
- Include an aggressive follow-up component for reluctant or tardy donor prospects; phonathons work well
- Inform donors about matching gift opportunities that might be available through their employers
- Personally thank donors for their generosity
- Report the results of the campaign to every donor and campaign worker

2. CAPITAL CAMPAIGNS

Your parish wants to build a new church, or add a parish center to its complex, or construct an auditorium for its school, or establish an endowment large enough to support one or more of its programs and services. You can wait until a generous parishioner wins the multistate powerball lottery and contributes 10 percent of the winnings, or you can conduct a capital campaign.

What you need to know about capital campaigns: Capital campaigns are "sometime things." Most parishes—indeed most nonprofit organizations—are hand-to-mouth operations which are either unable or unwilling to incorporate line items such as "depreciation" or "capital fund" accounts into their operating budgets. (Such accounts impose a discipline on an organization to accumulate funds for major building projects and equipment replacement.) Consequently, from time to time, parish needs outstrip financial resources, thereby creating the climate for a capital campaign.

The decision to launch a capital campaign is the most vexatious and demanding of all stewardship of treasure fund-raising enterprises. A capital campaign requires the complete and unequivocal support of an organization's leadership, meticulous planning, and heavy volunteer involvement.

Most parish capital campaigns are "bricks-and-mortar" fund-raising events for new buildings, renovations, major equipment, and so on. Happily, however, a growing number of dioceses are following the lead of universities, hospitals, and other development pioneers by creating foundations to encourage and facilitate capital campaigns for parish, school, and diocesan endowments. These foundations are already having a profound positive impact on the financial future of the Catholic Church in the United States (see Chapter 14).

Capital campaigns are indeed daunting, but should not be avoided for that reason. When properly managed, they touch a level of philanthropic generosity that no other fund-raising tactic can match. Two words capture the essence of every element necessary for a fruitful capital campaign: preparation and ownership. If parish or diocesan leaders do their homework, and if all parishioners truly *own* the campaign, success is guaranteed.

An early question that must be answered is this: Should outside professional consultation be engaged for the campaign? There are two capital campaign elements for which fund-raising consultants are typically hired: (1) to conduct a feasibility study; and (2) to direct the campaign itself.

A feasibility study consists of numerous interviews with key members of the community to determine the level of support for a proposed capital campaign. A competent feasibility study will also identify donor prospects who are willing to consider sizable campaign contributions.

Professional campaign management involves organizing the campaign, setting and "riding herd" on a timetable, generating materials, establishing a record-keeping system, providing training for volunteer solicitors, monitoring the campaign's progress, and so on. Parish or diocesan leaders should not think that by employing fund-raising counsel they can just sit back and watch the money roll in; they will still be heavily involved in much of the work of the campaign under the direction of the professional campaign manager.

Fund-raising consultants—many of whom are quite reputable—are, first and foremost, salespersons working for-profit businesses. Their ultimate task is to sell you their services. Choosing outside fund-raising counsel should be approached with a healthy dose of caveat emptor.

Remember: you're interested in *results*, not promises. You want a consultant to assist in setting a realistic campaign goal (a reliable feasibility study will do that), and help volunteer campaign committees reach that goal. Hiring a fund-raising consultant will *not* guarantee a successful campaign. Money will certainly be raised, but, for any number of different reasons, your campaign goal may not be achieved. Consultants typically receive their full fees regardless of the outcome of the campaign. (See "Do-It-Yourself or Hire a Pro?" in Chapter 17.)

(NOTE: Some diocesan stewardship and development offices provide capital campaign consultation as a service for their own parishes, schools, and other organizations. Most parishes and Catholic schools have enough competent volunteer manpower to conduct their own capital campaigns, with some advice and guidance from their diocesan development or stewardship offices.)

What you need to have to conduct a capital campaign: Here are some essential preparatory steps that need to be in place in the conduct of a capital campaign:

- Excellent Case Statement: A case statement is a printed brochure or small booklet with three components: (1) brief history of the parish; (2) review of current status of parish life; and (3) future outlook for the parish including detailed description of the project for which the capital campaign will be conducted

- Enthusiastic support from the top. The key word is *enthusiastic.* Pastor and parish leaders must be vocal cheerleaders for the project.
- Ownership by the entire parish
- Parishioners must agree on the project's value for the parish and accept responsibility for the campaign
- Accurate parishioner records/information; records should include former parishioners and/or parish school alumni who have moved away; donor prospects should be divided into suggested giving levels
- Trained and motivated volunteer solicitors
- Strong administrative support throughout the campaign
- Realistic budget
- Clear timetable with absolute deadlines
- Professional consultation, if needed
- "Go-to" chairperson(s) or campaign manager
- Well-organized, trained, and motivated campaign cabinet
- High-quality communications network and plan

How to create ownership and support for a capital campaign: These efforts must be consistent before, during, and after any capital campaign. Before a campaign starts, the following elements are necessary:

- *Listen, listen, listen* (1) Conduct parish-wide surveys and town hall meetings to solicit input about parish needs; discuss reasons for a capital campaign at this time. (2) Before making any campaign plans, meet with all leadership organizations (parish council, finance committee, school board, and so on) and other influential parish groups to explain the need for the campaign, to elicit their input, and to confirm their approval and support.
- *Communicate, communicate, communicate!* (1) Explain the campaign's project to key parish leadership groups with as much detail as possible. (2) Announce the project to the entire parish with a flourish and a positive attitude. (3) Provide frequent updates on the status of the preparations for the campaign and project.

- *Prepare, prepare, prepare!* (1) Train solicitors. Use role-playing to practice asking for and receiving pledges. (2) Create all necessary materials: case statement, pledge cards, gift receipts, self-addressed return envelopes, and so on. (3) Thoroughly research companies and businesses which may match their employees' charitable gifts, and other corporate or foundation grant-making organizations. Don't be discouraged when you discover that many corporations with charitable gift budgets will not give to religious groups or causes. (See the section on grants that follows.)

During a capital campaign, the following elements come to the forefront:

- *Support, support, support!* (1) Make volunteer divisions small enough to allow for maximum interaction between subcommittee captains and their solicitation teams. (2) Provide immediate responsive service for volunteer workers as needed; be sure each worker has a designated "go-to" person to contact about any questions or difficulties.
- *Ask, ask, ask!* (1) Personally solicit major donor prospects before beginning the general campaign for the entire community. Fundraising wisdom says that as much as 90 percent of a capital campaign's contributions can come from as few as 10 percent of the organization's donor prospects. It's advisable to have at least 50 percent of the campaign goal already committed before the general campaign kicks off. (2) Structure campaign organization so that as many donor prospects as possible are personally solicited for their pledges. (3) Ask for *pledges*, not gifts or contributions. (4) When direct mail is used, follow the rules. (See the section on direct mail that follows.)

One requirement is most important following a capital campaign:

- *Thank, thank, thank!* (1) Personally thank donors for their generosity *within two or three days after their pledges have been received.* (2) Publicly thank everyone whose gifts of time and talent contributed to the campaign's success.

Capital campaigns within a total stewardship context: Parishes which have taken the leap of faith into total stewardship may never be faced with the need to conduct a capital campaign. In a parish where the majority of parish members are tithing or giving proportionately, ordinary income should greatly exceed expenses, thereby allowing the parish to accumulate enough reserve funds to cover most extraordinary capital needs. When a capital campaign is required, tithing parishioners should be encouraged to make their pledges from their "4 percent to other worthy causes" already mentioned above in the discussion about tithing.

3. DIRECT MAIL

The president of a nonprofit organization's board of directors says to her fellow board members: "We need more money to cover our operating expenses this year. I'll send a letter to our donors and ask them to increase their giving."

The executive director of a charitable agency says to his development director: "We need to expand our donor base. Get a list of all the wealthy people in our area who are not donors. Send them one of our brochures and a letter asking them to give to our organization."

These two brief scenarios contain some of the best and worst elements of direct-mail fund-raising, which is perhaps the most risky of all fund-raising strategies.

What you need to know about direct mail: Direct mail fund-raising is much more than just "sending a letter to ask for money." To professional fund-raisers, it's a highly specialized discipline requiring extremely sophisticated techniques, talents, and equipment. It can be totally cost-inefficient and should therefore be approached with extreme caution.

If a parish, school, diocese, or other Catholic organization is not familiar with such things as list rentals, package testing, the DMMA, and so on, it should not attempt to use direct mail as a means of acquiring new donors. If, on the other hand, an organization wants to communicate with or solicit its own members, direct mail can be an effective tool, *but only if used correctly.*

The direct-mail industry is pervasive and highly specialized. Every American household is acquainted with direct-mail promotions and solicitations; they're stuffed in our mailboxes almost daily. Whenever a parish or diocese uses the postal service to communicate with parishioners or solicit contributions, they're competing with some of the foremost marketing experts in the United States, people who work for high-powered corporations, national charities, universities, hospitals, political fund-raising companies, and so on.

One of the best ways to assess the level of creative talent employed by direct mailers is by analyzing the direct-mail pieces that regularly appear in your own mail box. Remember: behind each direct mail "package" is a team of highly skilled professional graphic artists, designers, copywriters, and marketing psychologists trying to find ways to separate you from some of your money.

It's also important to know that direct-mail specialists use extremely sophisticated technological marketing instruments. For example, direct-mail marketing professionals have access to information about each American household from gargantuan data collection services that make George Orwell's "Big Brother" seem more like "Little Third Cousin by Marriage!"

To some marketing professionals, people are just a series of numbers: social security, credit cards, bank accounts, telephones, zip codes, and so on. Whenever we perform a transaction using one of our numbers, that transaction becomes part of our "permanent record" which can be accessed by several consumer data collection services. These services can supply marketers with reports about every American consumer, reports which are loaded with information about buying, spending, and saving habits, values, interests, desires, and so on. From this information, direct mail and other marketers determine personal "hot buttons," then design marketing materials to push those buttons.

As you review the marketing mail you receive each week, watch for evidence of this information in the hands of those who created each direct-mail piece.

What you need to have to conduct a direct-mail campaign: Take into account these essentials for running a direct-mail campaign:

- Up-to-date computer hardware with plenty of memory
- Computer printer that quickly prints letter-quality documents and has envelope-feed capabilities
- Advanced computer software including a word processor whose capabilities staff members can use (particularly for merging and personalizing letters), and a donor data base/record-keeping program which is faithfully kept current

- Talented people with the skills to design persuasive direct mail packages; these could be staff members, parish volunteers, or persons hired through a reputable local marketing or advertising agency
- Staff members or hired marketing consultants with extensive direct mail marketing experience
- Adequate, realistic budget
- As much information as possible about your "target" groups
- The basic direct-mail fund-raising package formula: (1) outside mailing envelope; (2) personalized letter; (3) reply device (something donors fill out and enclose with their contribution); (4) return envelope.

(NOTE: Much has already been published and continues to be written about direct-mail fund-raising. For more extensive information consult the references in the Bibliography.)

What you need to do to conduct a direct-mail campaign: Since parishes and dioceses must occasionally use the mail to raise money, it's important to remember that each direct-mail solicitation will be placed in parishioners' mailboxes alongside professionally created pieces that silently scream for their attention. The first goal of any direct-mail package is to be opened and read. The second goal is to motivate the prospective donor to take action, which means filling out the reply device and sending it with a contribution check in the return envelope.

Here are a few "dos and don'ts" to consider when preparing the four basic items of a direct-mail solicitation. Advice for creating an effective mailing envelope is as follows:

- Mail first-class
- Use the largest possible "live" stamp
- Type or print donor prospects' names directly on the envelope (no labels or window envelopes)
- Odd-sized envelopes are more intriguing than standard #10's and are more likely to be opened
- "Teaser" copy on the envelope is a good idea, but only if it is *very* compelling

Some aspects of the direct-mail letter that ought to be considered are these:

- Date the letter, and mail it on that date
- Personalize the salutation and add one or two personalized references in the body of the letter; be careful not to overuse this technique, and make sure each personalization is accurate
- Letters should be individually typed or printed
- Keep sentences, paragraphs and letters short; ordinarily, fundraising letters should be only one page; letters that tell an interesting story, however, can be longer
- Use at least 10-point serif type (it's easier to read)
- Tell a story; add feelings/emotions; humor is rarely if ever appropriate
- A P.S. is almost always read, so use it judiciously
- Begin the letter with a powerful "grabber"
- Ask for specific action and gift; stress urgency
- Thank former donors for their previous generosity; mention amount of previous gift/pledge
- Test several letters on donor volunteers before making a final selection
- If asking for a pledge, do not use words like *gift* or *contribution*

Considerations for constructing the reply device include the following:

- Be sure there is adequate space for donors to fill in names and addresses; even better would be names and addresses preprinted on the device
- Use check boxes as much as possible; your goal is to make it as easy as possible for donors to give
- Tell donors how to make out personal checks, and where to send them
- If using recommended gift amounts (for example, $1,000, $500, $250, and so on), put the highest amount first, but add a fill-in space before the highest amount and after the lowest amount

When constructing the return envelope in a direct-mail campaign, the following should be taken into account:

- Use business-reply envelopes (BRE's); yes, there is an extra expense (ask your local post office for details), but a larger return will more than offset the cost
- Make reply envelopes large enough to accept business-size checks plus the reply device without folding them
- An effective alternative to BRE's is placing a live first-class stamp on a plain, preaddressed return envelope; be careful: some donors may find this wasteful
- Be wary of fancy tear-and-fold-and-seal return mailing envelopes and reply devices: many elderly donors find them too confusing to use

A final rule of thumb: The goal of direct-mail soliciting is to raise as much money as possible for a parish or diocese. Every aspect of every package should be designed with donor prospects in mind. Winning awards for attractive materials, graphic designs, copywriting, and so on, may make fundraisers feel good, but the true measure of direct-mail effectiveness is its productivity. The most successful direct-mail pieces are created by people who truly know and respect their donors.

4. ESTATE PLANNING/DEFERRED GIFTS

How many funerals are conducted each year in your parish? How many deaths are reported each year among the alumni of your Catholic school? How many of these deceased individuals included a charitable bequest in their wills? If your answer to the latter question is either "none" or "very few," your parish, school, or other favorite charity, as well as its deceased members or supporters, are missing superb opportunities for gifts that can make a real difference.

Social economists tell us we're entering an era of enormous transfer of wealth from one generation to the next. As baby boomers progress into their senior years, the asset-transfer phenomenon will become massive. A charitable entity that neglects to take advantage of the philanthropic possibilities created by this watershed event is doing a disservice both to its living constituents, who benefit from its programs and services, and to its deceased supporters who die ignorant of the chance to do something special for themselves and for the organization that meant so much to them during their lifetimes. That "something special" may be a charitable contribution of a magnitude they were unable to accomplish while they were alive.

For example, what if 10 percent of a parish's deceased parishioners had been thoughtful enough to include the parish in their wills?—or 25 percent?—or 50 percent? The results would be astonishing! For most charitable organizations, promoting wills and bequests is a typical first step into the somewhat intimidating fund-raising arena known as estate planning.

Many nonprofit organizations have long recognized the enormous philanthropic potential of a fully functioning estate planning program. Catholic charitable organizations have been noticeably slow to embrace this most fruitful of all fund-raising specialties. But the "times they are a-changing." Catholic dioceses, parishes, and schools are hastening to add estate planning components to their stewardship of treasure menus!

What you need to know about planned gifts: Deferred gifts are those charitable and other gifts which are put off until a later time in a person's life and/or until after a person's death. Estate planning refers to a combination of legal and financial strategies by which a person organizes his or her assets and possessions for future contingencies.

Here is a brief overview and analysis of the traditional deferred giving/ estate planning instruments:

A. Wills

A will is a legal document which outlines and directs the disposition of a person's possessions upon that person's death. One of the simplest ways a donor can make a substantial gift to a favorite charitable organization is through a bequest in a will. A bequest is giving or leaving something to someone by means of a will.

In addition to the inevitability of death, there's another reality associated with dying for most of us: our assets can be converted into cash. For this reason, many donors can make much larger contributions to their parishes, dioceses, Catholic schools, or other charitable entities by means of bequests than they could ever hope to make during their lifetimes.

Researchers tell us that most adults do not have a will. Because each state has made provisions for its citizens who die intestate (that is, without a will), it's entirely possible that a state's "will" may work well for certain individuals. If, on the other hand, a person wants to exercise control over the distribution of his or her assets after death, including charitable bequests, a will is absolutely necessary. No state law permits charitable gifts after death without a will. In addition, any pledge to make charitable contributions ceases with the death of the donor; such a pledge can be continued only if a provision has been included in the donor's will.

There are several common types of charitable bequests:

- Specific dollar amount
- Particular items of property such as real estate, stocks, heirlooms, and so on
- Percentage of assets
- Residue: whatever is left after all other obligations have been met
- A combination of the above
- A charitable gift which provides life income for one or more beneficiaries

Many dioceses offer a "Wills Seminar" service for parishes and other Catholic organizations. It's a wise parish leader who schedules at least one Wills Seminar each year for parishioners. (See Appendix 11 which outlines the content of a wills seminar.)

B. Gift Annuity

A gift annuity is a private agreement between a donor and a charitable organization whereby the donor transfers assets to a charity in return for which the charity agrees to provide annual or more frequent income payments to the donor or other beneficiaries until their deaths. Income payment amounts are usually based on actuarial tables created by an organization known as the Committee on Gift Annuities. Charities invest donors' initial gifts—the "principal"—and attempt to earn as much income as possible to help meet their payment obligations to donors. Upon the deaths of the beneficiaries, the remaining principal becomes the property of the charitable organizations.

Gift annuities create attractive income and tax advantages for donors and hold the promise of potentially large future contributions for charitable organizations. The biggest risk, however, belongs to the charity. If donors live beyond their life expectancies, the agreed-upon payments must still be honored. In other words, donor longevity could result not only in eventual depletion of the principal, but could also drain the organization's other assets.

C. Pooled Income Fund

This vehicle could be described as a "mutual fund for donors." A pooled income fund is a legal entity, established according to specific IRS guidelines, which a charitable organization can use to attract contributions. Donors transfer assets to the organization's pooled income fund. The assets from all donors are "pooled" and become the fund's principal. The charity, usually with professional advice, invests the principal. Donors or other designated beneficiaries receive annual or more frequent income payments based on the fund's earnings and the donors' portion of the principal. Upon the deaths of all beneficiaries of a particular gift to the pooled income fund, that gift's portion of the fund's principal becomes a contribution to the charitable organization.

Pooled income funds are especially appealing to donors with smaller amounts to contribute. PIF tax advantages are quite attractive when donors transfer highly appreciated securities (for example, stocks which were purchased several years ago for fifteen dollars per share and are now selling for fifty dollars per share).

The legalities of creating and administering a pooled income fund are complicated and generally exceed the capabilities of smaller organizations such as parishes or individual Catholic schools. A *diocesan* pooled income fund, however, is a marvelous vehicle by which a diocese can serve its parishes, schools and other organizations.

D. Life Estate Agreement

This arrangement ordinarily involves donors who want to transfer ownership of their home or other real estate to a charity—which produces tax advantages—while retaining the right to live in the donated home or use the real estate until death. When the life tenants die (the original donors or other beneficiaries), the charity usually sells the property and thereby receives a substantial cash contribution. There are a few issues that must be considered when entering into a life estate agreement such as income produced by the property, taxes, value of the property, depreciation, and so on. Nevertheless, life estate agreements are generally fairly simple to structure and administer, and their benefits outweigh any drawbacks. Charities should, however, be sure to investigate thoroughly the environmental and taxation status of all real estate before accepting it as a gift or potential gift.

E. Charitable Lead Trust

This seldom-used strategy could be described as a type of loan of a donor's assets to a qualified charitable organization. A donor places assets in a trust—usually a temporary arrangement—which become the trust's principal. The charity, not the donor, receives the income generated by the trust during its existence. This income must be reported by the donor as taxable income. When the trust terminates, the principal is returned to the donor or to another named beneficiary. Tax advantages for the donor are limited to an income-tax deduction determined at the time the assets are placed in the trust, provided that the terms of the trust meet IRS requirements. The charity, on the other hand, receives income for the duration of the trust and *could* become the beneficiary of the principal upon the death of the donor.

F. Revocable Charitable Trust

As suggested by its name, this giving plan involves donors who place assets in a trust which can be terminated upon the donors' demand. All or a portion of the net income from the trust is paid to charitable or noncharitable organizations according to the donors' wishes. Financial advantages for donors are quite limited. Charitable organizations named in the trust could receive all or a portion of the assets upon the death of the last donor beneficiary at the discretion of the donors.

G. Charitable Remainder Annuity Trust (CRAT)/ Charitable Remainder Unitrust (CRUT)

CRATs and CRUTs are similar types of entities. They differ in the manner in which income payments to donors are determined. CRUTs and CRATs involve donors placing assets in a trust irrevocably. Donor-designated beneficiaries receive income from the trust for life. Upon their deaths, the remaining principal goes to the charity.

Income paid to beneficiaries of a CRAT is an agreed-upon percentage of the initial net fair market value of the principal, or a specific amount of money. Income paid to CRUT beneficiaries is an agreed-upon percentage of the net fair market value of the principal, valued annually. CRAT or CRUT payments to donors (or other beneficiaries named in the original agreement) must be made at least annually, but may be made more frequently.

Tax advantages for donors include the following:

- An initial income tax deduction
- Avoiding capital gains (transferring highly appreciated assets is strongly recommended!)
- Savings on federal estate taxes

As with other similar arrangements that have been described thus far, the charity receives the assets of the trust at the death of the final income beneficiary.

H. Life Insurance

There are two common ways to use life insurance policies for charitable purposes. The simplest method is to name a favorite charity as the policy's beneficiary. This technique does have some estate tax benefits. A second method, although somewhat more complicated, has an attractive lifetime tax advantage. This strategy involves a donor who purchases a life insurance policy on his or her life, then transfers ownership of the policy to a favorite charity. The charity is responsible for paying the premiums, but the donor makes a charitable contribution equal to the cost of the premiums each time they are due, thereby receiving a charitable contribution tax deduction.

Another increasingly popular use of insurance involves coupling a life insurance policy with a trust and a charitable bequest. This strategy—often referred to as a "charitable gift/wealth replacement plan"—is employed as a means of providing a donor's heirs with the same inheritance they would have received before the charitable bequest was made. (NOTE: Charitable organizations should always remember that when they become involved with a potential donor's assets, somewhere there are heirs with a vested interest. The greater the assets, the more intense the interest!) Because of the complicated nature of a charitable gift/wealth replacement plan, donors are well advised to seek competent professional help.

It should be noted that the rules of the taxation game are constantly changing as federal and state governments forever seek ways to enhance their revenue (read: "get more tax dollars"). For this and other reasons, it should be abundantly obvious from our brief treatment of these common estate planning devices that competent legal and financial assistance is *always* advisable.

What you need to have to solicit planned gifts: Here are some earmarks of a solicitation campaign for planned and deferred gifts.

- A long-term view—a parish and the people it serves will reap great future benefits from current estate planning efforts
- Well-written, attractive, informative, and accurate printed materials
- Highly developed awareness of the estate planning possibilities and opportunities for an organization and its supporters
- Excellent vehicles of communication, both verbal and written
- Regularly scheduled series of wills and estate planning seminars
- Heavy involvement of legal and financial professionals who are parishioners: attorneys, bankers, accountants, stock brokers, financial planners, and so on
- Competent financial and legal consultation to oversee all aspects of the organization's estate planning program

What you need to do to take advantage of planned gifts: Two words summarize everything that is needed for a successful and productive estate planning enterprise: *education* and *communication.*

Education. As already noted, estate planning, and its philanthropic cousin, deferred giving, can be enormously complicated items on a parish's fund-raising menu. Most parishioners are ignorant of, and intimidated by, the legal and financial twists and turns associated with each of these highly specialized financial planning mechanisms. Consequently, most parishioners greatly appreciate parish efforts to help them organize their financial affairs.

For this reason, stewardship parishes should provide regular opportunities for parishioners to learn more about the benefits of a competent and comprehensive estate plan through occasional (two to three per year) wills seminars and estate planning workshops, supplemented with readily available printed information.

Communication. In addition to formal education and training programs, parishes should incorporate estate planning information into their communication networks. Newsletter articles, parish bulletin "blurbs," posters, and direct-mailed financial planning flyers are just a few of the ways to keep estate planning and deferred giving in parishioners' "top-of-mind awareness." Occasional announcements at the end of Mass and during selected parish gatherings are also ways to promote parish estate planning endeavors. Many parishes are creating planned giving donor recognition societies (see Chapter 15) as excellent vehicles for encouraging parishioners to include their parishes in their estate plans.

5. CORPORATE, FOUNDATION, AND GOVERNMENT GRANTS

Diocesan stewardship and development directors are frequently approached by pastors or school principals or nonprofit board members asking variations of this question: "Can we find some grants for (place any project or organization's name here)?" The painful answer in almost every case is "No." It is true that thousands of foundations and corporations, as well as government entities, give billions of dollars in grants to nonprofit organizations each year. However, it is also true that thousands of nonprofit organizations generate millions of grant requests each year. It is further true that grant-making organizations usually have very specific guidelines and spheres of interest—both programmatic and geographic—which determine how their dollars are distributed. It is even further true that grants are rarely given for a nonprofit organization's operating expenses. In other words, seeking grant money is a huge, time-consuming gamble which is replete with disappointments.

With these thoughts in mind, we offer the following information and tips about grant-seeking.

What you need to know about obtaining grants: Successful grant-proposal writing can be summed up in three words: *preparation, precision, and persistence.*

(1) *Preparation*: The first, absolutely essential and most difficult step in the grant-seeking process is to have a project which is truly deserving of consideration for funding. The next step is to identify those foundations whose funding parameters match the proposed project. This is accomplished by researching the following information about each foundation:

- Size and status of assets
- Types of grants and to whom they are given

- Name and address of current contact person
- Guidelines for submitting proposals
- Names of board members
- Size-ranges of grants

This material can be obtained through several sources. A diocesan office of stewardship or development should be the first stop for a parish, school, or other Catholic organization. Next, a local public library may have access to the wealth of information accumulated and updated each year by the Foundation Center in New York City. In addition, many central libraries in major metropolitan areas are repositories for the most recent tax records of private foundations located within their respective states. Finally, nonprofit donor alliances in many states annually compile, update, publish, and sell foundation directories containing all of the information listed above for the private foundations within their states.

(2) Precision: After possible funding sources have been located, the next step is to develop individual grant proposals. For this phase of the process, it's vitally important to follow precisely all grant proposal guidelines publicized by the foundations selected to receive proposals. It's equally critical to personalize and tailor each proposal to the targeted foundations, based on the information that was discovered in the homework phase.

(3) Persistence: The odds of receiving funding for an attractive project are increased by how carefully the homework and precision phases are carried out. But the competition for foundation grants is intense, which means that the vast majority of proposals will receive terse but kind letters of declination. Fund-raising neophytes are usually discouraged by these "thanks, but no thanks" letters. Experienced development old-timers, on the other hand, immediately look for clues that indicate that the proposal might be resubmitted for consideration at a later date. As a general rule, unless a foundation's refusal letter indicates that the proposed project is *forever* totally unfundable, it may be eligible for another look during the foundation's next fiscal year. In other words, "No, thanks" does not necessarily mean "Never, thanks."

Big Guys and Little Guys: Thorough homework will disclose an important distinction in the grant-making world. There are two groups of foundations: big guys and little guys. Big guys have large assets and full-time paid staff members. Little guys have smaller assets and no—or few—paid staff members. Knowing this distinction is necessary because it impacts the manner in which you approach each group for funding. Here are a few insights which may be helpful.

(1) Large foundations tend to be more systematic and structured in their approach to grant-making decisions; small foundations are generally more informal in their operations and often less specific regarding what they will and will not fund, what they require in proposals, deadlines, and so on.

(2) Large foundations shy away from bricks-and-mortar projects in favor of innovative services and cutting-edge programs; small foundations are more inclined to fund anything their decision-makers think is worthwhile.

(3) Large foundations have more elaborate screening procedures; proposals may pass through several bureaucratic layers before final decisions are made. Small foundations are more closely controlled by the individual, family, or company executives who initially established the foundation; funding decisions are made by one person or a few foundation officers.

(4) Most large foundations have few if any geographic limitations for funding requests; they will consider national or even international projects. Small foundations tend to fund proposals which benefit people or organizations close to home.

(5) Large foundations typically make grant decisions based primarily on the merits of proposals. Officers of small foundations may consider a proposal's worthiness, but they are also likely to fund favorite projects of board members or proposals submitted by organizations which are recommended by trusted friends or colleagues of board members.

(6) Most foundations—large and small—are reluctant to make grants to denominational religious organizations because of the potential flood of requests they would receive. There are, however, a number of private foundations which concentrate their grant awards on specific religious groups. (See Chapter 20, "References and Resources.") Furthermore, grants to private (read: "Catholic") schools are becoming increasingly popular due to the favorable publicity Catholic education has been receiving in recent years.

(7) Seeking foundation support for ordinary operating expenses is generally wasted effort. Foundations, large and small, prefer making grants for time-limited projects. Should a grant for operating funds be approved, it, too, will typically be limited to a short time period: no more than two or three years.

(8) By law, foundations are required to distribute at least 5 percent of their assets each year. This means that, in favorable investment years, many foundations will have more money to distribute for worthy grants.

What you need to have to obtain grants:

- A fundable project or need that will truly "make a difference" in the life of the parish or surrounding community
- Clearly written, concise, well-organized grant proposals
- If possible, parishioners or members who have established relationships with any of the funding source's decision-makers

What you need to do to obtain grants:

- Practice patience. Some foundations are slow to respond to requests for funding; if you know a proposal has indeed been received (sending it by certified mail gets you a receipt), just sit tight and wait.
- Personalize everything; don't send "To Whom It May Concern" or "Dear Sir or Madam" proposals.
- Send just a few proposals (three to five) to foundations whose funding patterns and geographic requirements seem to match the project. Do not send "shotgun" proposals to twenty or thirty foundations. Many foundation officers are acquainted with one another; they will know who has done their homework and who hasn't.
- Neat and accurate counts! Think about the person who will receive the proposal. If his or her initial visual impression is negative, the proposal will most likely go no further toward a funding decision.
- The cover letter for a proposal should be no longer than one page with a *very brief* description of the proposed project and its cost; it should be signed by the organization's highest official and/or by its most influential volunteer, or both.
- Don't forget to include information that verifies the requesting organization's nonprofit status.
- Personal visits with foundation officers are usually not necessary or even helpful. If, however, a visit is required or requested, send the organization's top person along with its top volunteer.
- If an organization is committed to seeking grants as an integral component of its fund-raising activities, one or more staff mem-

bers should attend a nearby Grantsmanship Center training program as soon as possible.

Additional Tips for Grant Proposals:

- Potential funding sources want to know how much the requesting organization will contribute to each proposed project. Be sure to include information in grant proposals about staff and financial resources the organization will donate to projects.
- Many foundation officers are intrigued by matching or "wrap-up" grants for worthy projects which are already mostly funded from other sources.
- Although it may not be expressly requested in grant proposal guidelines, foundation officials are always curious about what will happen to a program or service when the grant money runs out. Anticipate this question with a plausible and acceptable response.
- If a project is funded, don't forget to thank the funding source. Even more important, don't forget to periodically inform the grant-maker about the project's status and impact.

Government Grants: The process for seeking government grants is quite different from what has already been described for private foundations. Although competition for government money is just as fierce as competition for private foundation grants, it's much more complicated. As one veteran grant writer observed: "Private foundation grant proposals are judged by their quality and content; government grant proposals are evaluated by weight and influence!"

Government grant monies generally target very specific needs. Many of the programs and projects which are created to meet these targeted needs originate from the dozens of office buildings surrounding Washington, D.C., which house the faceless, infamous corps of bureaucratic consultants often referred to as the "Beltway Bandits." Rarely, if ever, would a Catholic parish or organization find a substantial source of government funds for any of its programs, services, or projects. A parish or other Catholic entity is well-advised not to waste time and energy searching for government grants.

6. MEMORIAL/HONOR GIFTS

Picture this scene: a Catholic client is sitting in her attorney's office formulating the details of her last will and testament. At one point in the conversation she says: "I'd like to do something special for my parish after I'm gone, so I want to leave five thousand dollars for Masses to be said in my parish for me and my family." The attorney, a staunch Methodist who cannot know what such a gift actually means for her client's parish, dutifully adds the request to the client's list of bequests and moves on to the next item. (We've already addressed the problems this type of bequest can create in Chapter 11 in the section on "Mass Stipends and Stole Fees.")

One marvelous way for a parish to counteract difficulties caused by excessive requests for Masses is by promoting Memorial and Honor Gifts. A well-managed Memorial and Honor Giving Program can be a welcome addition to an organization's stewardship of treasure fund-raising menu.

What you need to know about Memorial/Honor Gifts: Memorial and honor gifts are specialized contributions to a parish, Catholic school, diocese, or any charitable organization.

A memorial gift is a simple yet thoughtful way to show respect and express sympathy when a friend or loved one dies. An honor gift is a marvelous means of celebrating notable events or milestones in the lives of friends or loved ones, such as birthdays, anniversaries, graduations, weddings, and so on.

Both donors and recipients like them because

- They satisfy a desire to do something special for a friend or loved one when a kind and considerate gesture is appropriate.
- Those whose lives they touch greatly appreciate them as gifts that continue to give through the good works they support.
- They help a parish, school, or other charitable organization continue important programs and services.
- They're confidential: the amount of the gift is never disclosed.
- They're noncompetitive: there's no need to "keep up with the Joneses" because they are confidential.
- They're tax-deductible.

Here's a step-by-step description of the memorial and honor gift process:

Step 1: The donor makes a contribution to a favorite religious, educational, or charitable organization in memory of someone who has died or in honor of someone celebrating a special event.

Step 2: The receiving organization records the following information:

- Name and address of donor
- Name and address of bereaved family or honored person(s)
- Name of deceased person or type of event or milestone
- Date of gift
- Amount of gift (never disclosed)

Step 3: Within twenty-four hours of receipt of a gift, the receiving organization prepares and mails the following:

- Personalized thank-you card to donor (including statement that the bereaved family or honored person(s) has (have) been notified
- Personalized gift-acknowledgment card to bereaved family or honored person(s)

Step 4: In the next issue of the organization's newsletter, the names of the deceased or honored person(s) are published, along with donors' names.

Step 5: One week after receiving the memorial or honor gift, the receiving organization sends a brief, personalized thank-you letter to the donor along with an official gift receipt and a copy of the organization's memorial/honor gift form.

What you need to have to solicit Memorial/Honor Gifts: A successful memorial and honor giving program requires an adequate supply of the following items, samples of some of which appear in Appendix 8:

- Promotional brochure explaining the mechanics of memorial and honor giving along with information about the parish, school, or organization
- Memorial/honor gift forms
- Donor thank-you cards and envelopes
- Memorial gift-acknowledgment cards and envelopes
- Honor gift-acknowledgment cards and envelopes
- Official gift receipts
- Systematic means of keeping accurate records

What you need to do to solicit Memorial/Honor Gifts: The success of memorial and honor giving is dependent on two factors: how well the program is administered, and how well it's promoted. Here are a few tips for both elements.

Proper Memorial/Honor Gift Administration:

1. Keep accurate records. Many donors will give only memorial and honor gifts to an organization. Consequently, it's wise to keep memorial and honor-giving records separate from other types of contributions to a parish or other organization.
2. Spell all names correctly. This is especially important since the names of donors and those they have memorialized or honored will be published.
3. Mail gift-acknowledgment cards promptly. Donors choose memorial and honor gifts because of a death or celebrated event. In both cases, donors want the notification of their gifts to be timely.
4. Be sure donors, bereaved families, and/or honored persons receive a copy of the newsletter in which their names appear.

How to Promote Memorial and Honor Giving: Memorial and honor gifts are not yet commonplace. A parish or other organization must, therefore, establish a continuing program of education and promotion about memorial and honor giving, and provide convenient ways for people to use them.

1. Be sure memorial/honor gift forms are readily available for parishioners, alumni, and so on.
2. Include memorial/honor gift forms in appropriate parish mailings.
3. Include regular promotional announcements in parish publications.
4. Send occasional special memorial/honor giving mailings to all parishioners, school families, and other constituents.
5. Ask area funeral directors to display parish memorial/honor gift forms when bereaved families request them.
6. "Piggyback" memorial and honor gift forms in parish mailings when possible and appropriate.

7. PHONATHONS

A phonathon is a fund-raising strategy that involves making phone calls to donor prospects to ask for their financial support. Nearly every American has experienced the relentless onslaught of the telemarketing industry. Is it any wonder, then, when a parish council member suggests a phonathon to raise money to meet a particular need, the other members may be merciless in their rejection of the idea?

Phonathons can be truly productive fund-raising events, but, by their very nature, they may legitimately be classified as telemarketing. If a phonathon is selected as a fund-raising option, every attempt must be made to distance it from the negative perceptions induced by some telemarketers.

Several professional telemarketing vendors have developed programs specifically designed for nonprofit organizations. For example, a few dioceses now use these services as a component of the follow-up phase for their annual appeals. If a telemarketing service is employed, the customer (parish or diocese) should clearly outline its expectations and closely monitor the calling procedures. A disastrous phonathon experience can create a fund-raising nightmare for an otherwise highly respected organization.

What you need to know about phonathons: Phonathons involve two groups of people: callers and "callees." A competently prepared phonathon carefully considers the nature of both groups in relationship to two key elements: *preparation* and *anticipation.* Both callers and donor prospects must be adequately *prepared.* This means thorough preservice training for callers. For prospects, preparation means establishing ample justification for the phonathon.

(1) Anticipation for callers requires training methods which address multiple "what-ifs." What if a donor prospect is hostile? What if the caller experiences eight ferocious hang-ups in a row, then finally makes contact with a prospect who is willing to listen? What if a prospect asks a question the caller can't answer? General guidelines and techniques for handling these and other "what ifs" should be included in caller training. However, since every possible situation cannot be anticipated before the phonathon takes place, qualified, experienced support persons must be available to assist callers during the phonathon.

(2) Anticipation for donor prospects is intensified through prephonathon communication and promotional activities. Every possible means should be employed to alert prospects to the impending phonathon, and to prepare them to receive their calls graciously and with a generous spirit. In a parish setting, anticipatory activities include articles in bulletins and newsletters, pulpit announcements, strategically placed posters, direct mail let-

ters/publications, and any other creative means of alerting parishioners that they will be solicited by phone, why they will be called, when it will happen, and what is expected of them.

When phonathons are conducted by parish volunteers, every effort should be made to ensure their comfort, convenience, and confidence. The atmosphere should be pleasant, almost partylike; snacks and refreshments should be provided. A location should be selected that lends itself to the task. An office with multiple phones and desks is ideal. (NOTE: Parishioners are excellent resource people for finding good phonathon locations such as bank branches, insurance or realty offices, and so on.) All pertinent information and materials should be prepared ahead of time. Individual callers should not be expected to make an inordinately large number of calls; ten to fifteen each is a reasonable range.

Prior to the phonathon event, donor prospects should be evaluated for their potential to contribute by sorting their pledge/calling cards into one of four categories: (1) Most Likely to Contribute; (2) Likely to Contribute; (3) Unsure; and (4) Unknown. The cards are then equally distributed to callers so that each volunteer has an equal chance for successful solicitations. Callers should be allowed to trade individual prospect cards if they believe they have more influence with certain prospects, or if they have reservations about speaking with particular persons.

What you need to have to conduct a successful phonathon:

- A strong, compelling case for soliciting money
- Accurate, up-to-date information about each donor prospect (giving history, family, relationship with the organization, and so on)
- Comfortable, pleasant location—(sufficient number of phones and outside lines, space for each caller to work, rest-room facilities, drinks—no alcohol—and snacks)
- Motivated, positive, well-trained callers (paid or volunteer)
- Call record forms which are easy to use
- Information sheet about the organization and the project for which funds are being raised
- Adequate support system before, during, and after the phonathon.
- Budget for such items as stationery/printing, postage, phone service (long distance, if necessary), refreshments, supplies, and other necessities
- Realistic, conversational scripts for callers, including suggestions

on how to handle objections and what to say when callers reach an answering machine
- Effective follow-up procedures

What you need to do before the phonathon:

- Prepare donors (see above)
- Cull donors who have already contributed (*a critical step*)
- Provide adequate training for callers as close as possible to the time of the actual event
- Carefully schedule each phase

What you need to do during the phonathon:

- Keep the atmosphere light
- Make the calling event a group activity. (This fosters a supportive atmosphere which helps to reinforce callers' confidence and motivation.)
- Keep distractions and background noise to a minimum
- *Avoid calling during the dinner hour*
- Be sure callers identify themselves as soon as they reach each prospect; if preevent communications and promotions were effective, prospects will be expecting the call

What you need to do following the phonathon:

- Follow-up all contributions/pledges immediately; don't forget the "thank-yous"
- For nondonors, send "Sorry you couldn't help at this time—maybe later" letter

8. SPECIAL EVENTS

Traditional special events fund-raisers include such diverse affairs as auctions, tribute dinners, celebrity or benefit performances, house tours, fashion shows, golf scrambles, black-tie galas, "Las Vegas" nights, seasonal festivals, food-tasting parties, car washes, roadblocks, and the oft maligned Catholic staple: bingo. The possibilities for special events are limited only by the creative imagination of an organization's staff members and volunteers. If there's any type of fund-raising for which committees were designed, it's special events.

However, special events are fraught with hazards which are often completely unknown or unexpected, and which no amount of planning can anticipate or overcome. Failures are commonplace. Here's a rule of thumb: do not be afraid to walk away from a special event that seems too precarious: it probably is!

What you need to know about special events: Here are a few general observations to help a parish, school, or other Catholic organization assess the relative merits of engaging in special-events fund-raising:

- The larger and more ambitious the event, the greater the risk; but the fund-raising potential is also greater.
- Special events demand strong, unswerving support from the organization's leadership.
- Many special events require massive amounts of volunteer help which can become overwhelming.
- Some special events necessitate substantial "up-front" financial investments which can be problematic for supporters (parishioners, alumni, board members, finance council members, parish council members, and so on). All successful fund-raising costs money. Special-events fund-raising is often quite expensive. Its cost effectiveness must be carefully and objectively weighed.
- A special event must match and captivate its target audience in order to be profitable.
- Some special events require specialized skills that staff members and/or volunteers may not possess; in these cases, it's wise to seek professional help.
- If a special event is selected primarily as a fund raiser, its focus should be on *raising as much money as possible.* All decisions should be made with this in mind.
- An organization must be especially conscious of the public image it wishes to present with a special event. This is especially meaningful when a secondary goal for an event is "friend-raising" to increase community awareness about the organization and to solidify donor support.
- Watch out! Donors may attend a fancy charity bash and assume they have made all of their contributions to an organization for the year! In that case, the organization loses.
- An organization that is planning to add an annual special event

to its fund-raising repertoire should avoid incorporating the revenue it generates into its regular operating budget. If, for some reason, the event is unsuccessful in any given year, it will not create an unnecessary financial hardship for the organization.

- Celebrity guest speakers or performers rarely appear *gratis*. Depending on the popularity and notoriety of a personality who is being considering for a special event, an organization's leaders should not be surprised if the celebrity's agent mentions a five- or even six-figure price tag for their famous client's appearance (a so-called "benefit performance" frequently benefits the performer more than the charity).

What you need to have to sponsor special events:

- Strong leadership support, and a talented, committed organizing team whose members are willing and able to give generously of their time and talent.
- Accurate understanding of who constitutes the event's target audience, and how to reach them.
- Well-organized, highly motivated volunteers who understand their roles, responsibilities, and goals.
- A comprehensive plan which includes a clear chain of command, schedule of deadlines, and a checklist of decisions and issues; here are a few sample items for the list:

___ indoors or outdoors (what about weather?)
___ food and refreshments
___ decorations
___ theme/logo
___ communications/publicity
___ tickets/sales
___ invitations
___ one-time or annual event?
___ programs
___ sponsors/underwriters
___ schedule/deadlines
___ venue/contracts
___ entertainment

- A designated team of knowledgeable troubleshooters who are strategically positioned and ready to help with any difficulty or emergency that arises during the event.
- A worst-case contingency plan.

What you need to do before the event:

- Plan, plan, plan. Populate a planning committee with a balance between left-brain organizers and right-brain dreamers.
- Work to keep costs as low as possible. This requires creativity, know-how, and a cadre of capable, influential contacts. Event-planners should try to secure as many donations as possible.
- Scan the special-events calendar in and around your organization's geographic area. What kind of competition might the event have in your community.
- Secure insurance and/or underwriting for large, risky events.
- Always be mindful of your target audience.

What you need to do during the event:

- Stress the importance of a value-added service mentality among all staff and volunteers.
- Keep an accurate record of everything associated with the event especially if it will be repeated.

What you need to do after the event:

- Conduct a no-holds-barred debriefing session with all volunteers and staff members. Solicit feedback about what worked, what didn't, and how the event could have been better.
- Follow-up with all appropriate thank-yous and kudos.
- Objectively evaluate the future of the event.

Summary: Here are ten basic elements for successful special events.

- Determine realistic expenses/income budget
- Get underwriting or sponsorship
- The event can't be boring; keep the program under control
- Set a strict timetable, and stick to it
- Make the best use of volunteers
- Maximize all publicity

- Keep accurate records
- Acknowledge contributors/show appreciation
- Make careful seating arrangements
- Get a prominent chairperson and strong, well-organized, clearly-defined committees

Here are common mistakes to avoid.

- Not thanking volunteers and contributors
- Not clearing the date of your event to avoid serious conflicts; avoid vacations and holidays
- Not getting union clearance when entertainment is involved
- Not knowing how much of the ticket price is tax deductible and how much is not
- Overselling an event, particularly show business events
- Not checking all technical equipment beforehand
- Not keeping accurate records

A final thought is appropriate here. There are three currently controversial issues which organizations must address when planning special events: (1) smoking; (2) use of alcohol; and (3) gambling. The dangers and emotional baggage of these issues are well documented. Event organizers for Catholic-sponsored events *must* weigh the physical, moral, and public relations pros and cons of all three topics.

CHAPTER 13

Treasure Renewals

In Chapter 4, we described the features of annual parish events referred to as "time and talent stewardship renewals." In this chapter we will touch on the components which are unique to parish stewardship of treasure renewals. We will not repeat the previous observations which apply to all stewardship renewals, so you may wish to review the earlier section before proceeding with the following commentary.

1. NECESSARY COMPONENTS AND MATERIALS

Here are the elements and materials that are recommended for a stewardship of treasure renewal program; examples of items marked with an asterisk can be found in Appendix 3.

- Calendar of events and activities*
- Bulletin inserts*
- Letters from the pastor and/or other parish leader(s)*
- Newsletter articles
- Promotional clip art
- Posters
- Prayers of the faithful
- Stewardship homilies
- Commitment reply form*
- Tithing formula/giving levels (See Appendix 4)
- Parish financial information

2. ISSUES AND CONCERNS

In addition to the general comments about stewardship renewals made earlier, here are several issues and concerns which apply specifically to stewardship of treasure renewals:

A. Confidentiality

Some parishioners may be reluctant to make a stewardship of treasure commitment in writing. One of their concerns is that unauthorized people may see their commitment card. One way to ensure confidentiality for stewardship of treasure commitments is to physically separate the dollars-and-cents portion of the commitment device from the name-and-address portion and return each to the parish separately. The stewardship of treasure commitment card sample in Appendix 3 was designed to preserve confidentiality by returning Part A and Part B in separate sealed envelopes.

A stewardship of treasure commitment is a private pact between a parishioner and God; no one other than God needs to know what a parishioner chooses to return to God in gratitude. Some parishes choose to demonstrate this personal agreement in dramatic fashion by publicly burning those portions of their members' commitment devices which contain the pledge amount. If the pledge amounts will be used for budgeting purposes (see below), don't forget to total them before setting the commitment cards on fire!

B. Parish Budgeting

Many parishes use the completed stewardship of treasure commitment cards to establish their income budget for the coming fiscal year. This is accomplished by totaling the annual amounts indicated on the commitment cards, then announcing the total to the parish as next year's projected income. Parish expenses are adjusted to the pledged income. If a substantial number of the commitment cards are returned (75 to 90 percent), the resulting income projection will generally be quite accurate and more than adequate.

C. Are Commitment Cards Legally Binding?

Parishioners occasionally wonder if completing and returning a stewardship of treasure commitment card legally binds them to fulfill their pledge. The answer is "no." Filling out a commitment card is nothing more than a good-faith promise made by a parishioner at a particular moment in time. Should his or her circumstances change, a parishioner is free to adjust the commitment.

CHAPTER 14

The Diocesan Foundation

One of the most exciting long-range fund-raising developments spreading throughout the United States is the diocesan foundation. The Catholic Church is somewhat of a Johnny-come-lately to this extremely useful and rewarding stewardship of treasure opportunity. Universities, hospitals, and many other charitable organizations have long recognized the extraordinary value of the foundation as a source of reliable operating income.

1. WHAT IS A DIOCESAN FOUNDATION?

Each diocesan foundation bears the unique stamp of the personality of the diocese that creates it, but most share these common characteristics and features.

- It's a charitable, nonprofit corporation which receives and holds resources that are called its corpus or principal.
- Its corpus is invested to produce income which, in turn, is distributed for general or specific charitable purposes.
- It's incorporated as a civil legal entity separate from the legal entity known as the diocese.
- In order to be in compliance with canon law, it remains under the jurisdiction of the local bishop.
- It serves parishes, schools and other diocesan entities by providing a simple means for establishing and building endowments.

2. WHAT ARE THE BENEFITS?

Diocesan foundations are attractive vehicles for donors as well as for dioceses, parishes, Catholic schools, and other Catholic organizations.

The benefits of a diocesan foundation for a diocese include:

- A pool of resources with unlimited potential for growth
- A reliable annual income for the programs, services and ministries of a diocese and its individual parishes, schools, and other entities
- A public statement about the diocese's commitment to its future financial security
- A means to attract donors to support the multitude of Christian works performed by and through the diocese

The benefits of a diocesan foundation for local entities (parishes, schools, and other organizations) include:

- Centralized pooling of resources for advantageous investing and cost-effective management
- Additional annual income for local programs and services
- Significant increase in local entities' abilities to attract major gifts

The benefits of a diocesan foundation for donors include:

- Attractive tax advantages, particularly through planned and deferred gifts
- A way for donors to ensure that their gifts will continue to give forever
- Gifts can be directed to help favorite diocesan or local organizations, institutions, and ministries

3. WHAT ARE ENDOWMENT FUNDS?

Endowment funds are an accumulation of resources that donors or organizations choose to maintain intact and in perpetuity; only the income from the funds is distributed for designated purposes. Typically, diocesan foundations function as receptacles for endowment funds which are contributed by parishes, schools, other organizations, or individual donors.

4. HOW DO DIOCESAN FOUNDATIONS OPERATE?

Most diocesan foundations are governed by a board of directors composed of lay and religious leaders. Usual foundation board subcommittees include:

- *Nominating:* establishes criteria for board membership; strives to match governance needs with available candidates; proposes slate of officers.
- *Bylaws:* prepares original governance documents; reviews and updates bylaws as needed.
- *Budget/finance:* provides oversight for the foundation's internal operating budget.
- *Investment:* determines investment policies for board approval; monitors all investment activities.
- *Distribution:* establishes income distribution formula and supervises all distributions to endowment holders.
- *Marketing:* formulates plan for promoting the foundation to its identified audiences.
- *Planned giving/estate planning:* develops and provides consultation services and educational programs designed to increase donor awareness regarding the importance of good estate planning.

5. WHAT'S THE DOWNSIDE OF DIOCESAN FOUNDATIONS?

Advantages associated with diocesan foundations far outweigh any disadvantages. It's important, however, to be cognizant of at least two potentially problematic issues:

A. Permanence

Resources used to create or add to an endowment's principal are no longer available for use by the endowing organization. Endowments are permanent and perpetual. Individuals and organizations create endowments to ensure the future of a particular ministry, program, item, or entity. A diocesan foundation is not a bank. It is, rather, a receptacle for endowments and other resources which will continue to generate funds for particular or general purposes forever.

When a parish establishes an endowment for any purpose, parish leaders must be totally aware of the fact that the endowment's principal must remain intact. Endowment funds can't be recalled next year, or next decade, or, indeed, next millennium, to pay for unforeseen or unusual capital expenses. To do so would completely destroy the trust that is the basis upon which endowments and foundations operate.

B. Vulnerability

A diocesan foundation's assets are part of the property of a diocese which, according to canon law, is ultimately controlled by a bishop. In the strictest interpretation of church law, a bishop can remove some or all of a foundation's assets and use them for purposes other than those for which they were intended. But, as already mentioned under "Permanence" on the previous page, the key issue is trust. Should an unwise bishop attempt to exercise his authority in this way, he would undoubtedly come into embarrassing public conflict with the foundation's board of directors and risk destroying forever the trust upon which a diocesan foundation is built. In the end, the foundation's assets would in all likelihood remain intact.

CHAPTER 15

Planned-Giving Societies

Among the most promising developments currently gaining momentum in Catholic parishes are planned giving societies. For much too long, dioceses, parishes, schools, and other Catholic entities have been content to operate in a precarious hand-to-mouth mode. This uncertain fiscal management style is beginning to change as dioceses create foundations which, among other things, serve their parishes, schools, and other entities by providing a simple vehicle for establishing and building endowments. Parishes, in turn, are creating planned-giving societies as a means of attracting funds for their endowments.

One can only fantasize about what the financial picture of the U.S. Catholic Church would look like today if, twenty-five or fifty years ago, dioceses and parishes had had the foresight and self-discipline to establish and build endowments for their operations!

1. ELEMENTS OF PLANNED-GIVING SOCIETIES

A planned-giving society is a donor recognition program which pays tribute to parishioners who have included a gift for a particular parish in their estate plans. The value and benefits of endowments have already been demonstrated (see Chapter 14). Creating and cultivating a parish planned giving society represents a giant step toward building endowments and other capital resources for the future. (NOTE: Some parishes may choose to offer planned-giving society membership to people who give single large gifts.) For Catholic parishes and schools, the potential for planned-giving societies is astounding!

In addition to identifying planned-gift donors, planned-giving societies are used to:

- Promote planned gifts
- Cultivate donor prospects
- Publicly acknowledge and thank donors
- Encourage continued giving (NOTE: Donors who include a gift for an organization in their estate plans tend to increase their lifetime giving to that organization due to a greater sense of ownership and affiliation.)

Criteria for membership include:

- Incorporating a bequest for the parish in a will
- Making a future gift to the parish through one or more of the usual planned giving vehicles: gift annuity, pooled income fund, charitable remainder trust, and so on
- Naming the parish as the beneficiary of an insurance policy

Donors can designate the use of their planned gifts for any of the following:

- *Unrestricted use:* parish leadership determines which needs are greatest and channel the funds to meet those needs
- *Restricted use:* donors specify the use of their gifts for certain favorite programs, services, or projects
- *Endowments:* donors request that their gifts be placed in a special endowment for general use or for a specific purpose

2. OPERATING A PLANNED-GIVING SOCIETY

The following are items and activities that are necessary for the successful operation of a planned-giving society:

- A name for the society that reflects the unique personality of the parish (a distinctive logo is also desirable)
- Attractive brochure and other promotional materials and literature. (See sample in Appendix 6.)
- Permanently displayed membership roster (plaque, giving tree)
- Occasional newsletter for society members; include articles about financial/estate planning

- Promote, promote, promote; examples include:
  — articles and advertisements in the church bulletin and parish newsletter
  — occasional reminder announcements from the pulpit
  — periodic special mailers to all parishioners and to targeted parishioners
  — strategically placed posters

- Treat members with special care; examples include:
  — hold special annual reception—not too fancy—for society members and parish leaders
  — send Christmas cards/birthday cards to members
  — list names of members in annual financial report
  — celebrate an annual Mass or prayer service honoring members

CHAPTER 16

Nontraditional Fund-Raising Sampler

Nonprofit fund-raisers are constantly searching for creative new ways to generate funds for their programs and services. At the same time, governmental entities are seeking to "enhance revenue" (read: "get more tax dollars"), and private sector business enterprises are working to increase their profits. Surprisingly, these diverse interests sometimes intersect in ways that create winners all around. Here are four examples of recently developed fund-raising strategies that not only create new income streams for charities, but in some cases produce tax revenues and profits.

1. AFFINITY CREDIT CARDS

An affinity credit card is a Visa or MasterCard issued to promote—and generate income for—a particular charitable institution or "cause." An affinity card is a normal credit card with a twist: each time it is used for a transaction, the affiliated charity earns a small percentage of the amount charged on the card. A substantial side benefit of an affinity card program is the public relations value gained by displaying the name of the charity each time its card is used.

Many universities and national charities sponsor affinity credit cards. Because banks and credit card companies operate with a profit motive, they prefer entering into affinity card arrangements with charitable organizations that possess large membership rosters. An individual parish, for example, would most likely not find a bank or credit card management company willing to administer an affinity card enterprise. On the other hand, a diocese, with the potential of delivering thousands of new credit card customers, may be a very attractive candidate for an affinity card program.

Since 1991, for example, the Catholic Diocese of Evansville in Indiana has promoted its own affinity card whose proceeds benefit diocesan Catholic schools. From the six thousand cards currently in use in that diocese, the Catholic schools realize more than fifty thousand dollars a year in royalty income.

There are several key issues which impact the success or failure of a diocesan affinity card program:

- It must be owned by local leaders. Pastors and other parish leaders must strongly support and endorse the program. This support cannot be assumed; it must be earned through communication and dialogue.
- Affinity cards must have no annual fee. A "no-annual-fee" feature is a bigger selling point to credit card customers than attractive percentage rates or any other card features.
- The royalty earned on each purchase—which must be negotiated with the issuing credit card company—should be reasonable and competitive. One-half of 1 percent royalty is recommended, although most credit card issuers will probably initially offer one-fourth of 1 percent.
- Marketing and promotion are critical elements; both the diocese and the credit card company must actively and aggressively participate.
- There should be no cost to the diocese except for staff time to initiate and promote the program, and minimal administration in receiving and disbursing royalty payments. The issuing credit card company should agree to provide attractive application and marketing materials including direct-mail promotions and advertisements in the diocesan newspaper. The diocese and its entities, on the other hand, must cooperate in a joint effort to encourage parishioners to apply for the cards and use them.
- Another important ingredient in the marketing mix is regular reporting to the widest possible audience regarding the income generated by the cards.

When an affinity card program is fully operational, it's an amazingly easy source of revenue for a charitable organization. Furthermore, the card-issuing company makes a profit on interest and merchant fees, and the government receive its share through taxes. Everybody wins!

One final caution may be in order concerning the revenue from affinity credit cards. Royalty payments from affinity cards may be considered unrelated business income and thereby subject to income tax. In Chapter 11, we discussed the Sierra Club affinity card court case which has been moving through the appeals process. At this writing, all judgments have been in favor of the Sierra Club, which means that affinity card royalty is not taxable income. However, it will probably be several more years before this issue reaches a final resolution.

2. SPECIAL GROUP LICENSE PLATES

Vanity license plates are popular items throughout the United States. In addition to providing motorists a means for making a value or lifestyle statement, or simply to bolster egos, vanity plates generate an additional source of state tax revenue. In recent years, states have expanded the vanity plate concept into the realm of fund-raising. Where state laws allow, any legitimate nonprofit organization can seek approval for its own special group recognition license plate. In many states, this trend began with colleges and universities that were allowed to display their names and logos on special license plates which their students and alumni could purchase.

Like vanity plates, special group plates cost more; there are usually two additional surcharges. One surcharge belongs to the state, the other is a contribution for the charitable organization whose name appears on the plate. When an organization submits an application to a state's bureau of motor vehicles for a special group plate, it must present proof that a minimum number of plates will be purchased in the first year that the plates are issued.

There are two obvious benefits which can be derived from special group plates:

- Additional source of operating revenue for the charity or "cause."
- Outstanding marketing and public relations value derived from hundreds or thousands of small, mobile billboards on the rear of cars traveling throughout the state and beyond.

There is, however, a serious downside to special group plates. Municipal, county, and state police departments are increasingly concerned about this rapidly growing fad. The burgeoning number of unique special group plates on U.S. streets and highways is causing difficulty for police officers who often need quickly to identify and trace license plates. Some states have either discontinued issuing special group plates or have temporarily suspended approving them.

3. PIGGYBACKING

A "piggyback" fund-raising strategy involves a charitable organization establishing a for-profit company whose profits are used to subsidize the nonprofit operation of the charity. One of the best known U.S. piggybacks is the Boston Pops Orchestra. The Boston Pops is a for-profit corporation that generates income through its enormously popular concerts, as well as from the sale of its recordings. These profits, in turn, are used to underwrite the budget of the nonprofit Boston Philharmonic Orchestra. The membership of both musical ensembles is practically identical! The conductor and musicians wear their Pops hats to make money, and they don their Philharmonic hats to spend it!

Many nonprofit hospitals operate for-profit gift shops. Nonprofit colleges and universities "sell" their team logos through lucrative for-profit agreements with clothing and specialty distributors.

Piggybacks do carry a certain amount of negative baggage. Nonprofit organizations have legitimately been accused of using their tax exempt status in order to compete unfairly with for-profit businesses. Furthermore, the issue of unrelated business income taxes (UBIT) can be most perplexing and potentially damaging to a charitable organization's reputation.

4. LONG-DISTANCE AFFINITY PROGRAMS

Another recent testimonial to the professional fund-raising community's almost limitless ingenuity are long-distance telephone affinity programs. These programs are a clever means of separating donors from some of their God-given treasure for charitable purposes. But they may also be a prime illustration of the consumer protection adage: "If it sounds too good to be true, it probably is!"

Since the early 1990s, long-distance affinity programs have been appearing and reappearing as a charitable fund-raising tactic. Charitable organizations of any size—including Catholic parishes and dioceses—receive a steady stream of proposals for such programs. These programs are made possible because major long-distance carriers, such as AT&T, Sprint, and MCI, prefer to remove themselves from the sales, promotion, and billing business. They allow smaller middleman companies to buy large blocks of long-distance service which they (the middlemen), in turn, sell to individuals and business customers.

The middleman providers have created a unique mechanism for identifying and signing up new customers. They seek alliances with nonprofit organizations, such as universities, religious organizations, and so on, with large membership or donor lists. Charitable organizations that agree to participate are asked to encourage their constituents to switch their long-distance carrier service to the middleman company. For this change, the charities receive a predetermined payback taken from the monthly long-distance bill of each new customer.

Here are some of the advantages of this fund-raising strategy.

- Depending on the size of its list, a nonprofit organization could receive a significant sum of new money for its programs and services.
- Some—but not all—of the middleman companies have good reputations for successful, high-integrity operations.
- Participating charities receive their portion of the program's income with minimal effort on their part.
- There are little or no out-of-pocket expenses for the participating charities.

Here are the disadvantages and caveats:

- The concept is still relatively speculative. Some of the service providers have no long-term history of success that would allay reasonable initial fears of potential nonprofit partners.
- In some cases, the actual long-distance carrier requires the middleman company not to tell potential customers who the true carrier is. This seems to imply that the major carriers may be unsure about the nature and future of these programs and don't want to risk the possibility that their reputations might be tarnished if problems arise.

- There are no guarantees about the future of the middleman companies. Many of the small companies that jumped into these programs in the early years have already failed. What happens to charities and their constituents who agreed to participate in such a scheme when it misfires?
- Established local and long-distance companies devote considerable time and resources to customer service training. Do the middleman companies provide the same high-quality customer service?
- Many of the middleman companies subcontract their billing operations to billing service providers. This proliferation of new services in such a high-tech industry raises questions about present and long-term service delivery and quality.
- The largest return from such a program for a nonprofit organization is realized by signing up high-volume business customers. Are businesses willing to change their long-distance carriers so that a particular nonprofit organization will receive a kickback? Why would a business not prefer to receive a comparable reduction in their current rates and then make a tax-deductible contribution to the charity?
- Most residential customers are already confused about long-distance services. Although the middleman companies tout lower rates for new customers, how long will these rates be in effect, and who controls them?
- Telephone customers currently deal with one or two companies for their telephone service. An affinity long-distance program would add at least two additional companies to this mix, thereby increasing the likelihood of "getting the run-around" when problems arise.
- It's likely that income received by a charitable organization from a long-distance affinity program would be considered unrelated business income by the IRS and would therefore be taxable.
- In many ways, the reputation and credibility of nonprofit organizations are placed in the hands of the middleman companies and their suppliers and subcontractors.

The burning question for charitable organizations which are considering long-distance affinity programs is: Do the financial benefits outweigh the potential risks?

CHAPTER 17

Odds and Ends

Here are several topics which should be incorporated into all discussions about what constitutes competent fund-raising by Catholic parishes, dioceses, and other charitable organizations.

1. DONOR RECORD-KEEPING

A parish is an extended spiritual family whose members, among other things, should be cared about and cared for. A parishioner has a right and a need to believe that "my parish knows me and loves me." The more parishioners feel attachment to, and ownership of, their parish, the more they will want to share their time, talent, and treasure.

One of the tools for creating and maintaining a welcoming, hospitable spirit in a parish is a well-constructed membership information database which addresses these two questions: (1) How much is currently known about each parishioner? (2) How much *should* be known about them? The answer to the latter question depends on several factors, but can probably be summarized with one additional question: What do parish leaders and staff members *need* to know in order to demonstrate to each parishioner that "my parish knows who I am?"

The benefits that can be derived from a superior membership information database are enormous. Communications with each parishioner can be highly personalized, thereby creating a greater sense of parish affiliation. Furthermore, professional staff members and volunteers will be better able to design and deliver programs and services to meet real needs of real people.

Here's a suggested checklist of information which a parish might use to design or select its database. The items are divided into three categories: (1) basic information; (2) advanced information; and (3) top-of-the-line information.

Basic information:

- Name(s), (individual, spouse, children)
- Nickname(s)
- Preferred title(s)
- Preferred salutation
- Address
- Place of work
- Marital status
- Home and work phone number(s)
- Anniversary date of membership
- Birthday(s)

Advanced information:

- Financial data (giving history: types of parish support—gift/number of pledges, cumulative annual and lifetime paid-to-date totals/balances, giving frequency, household income, and so on)
- Parish involvement (committee memberships, volunteer activities, ministries, and so on)
- Fax number
- E-mail address
- Church attendance history
- Hobbies/interests/skills/talents
- Educational history
- Vacation home address/phone number
- Civic involvement
- Cultural/sports interests
- Political affiliation
- Extended family information (parents, grandparents, grandchildren)

Top-of-the-line information:

- Directions to home
- Directions to place of work

- Personal income/wealth
- Tither (yes or no)?
- Cellular phone number
- Pager number
- Automatic generation of year-end tax information
- Is the parish included in the member's estate plan? If so, how?
- Close friends/personal contacts
- Notes from personal encounters
- Comments from others (staff members, friends, and so on)

NOTE: There are numerous computer programs on the market which are capable of handling parish information needs. A review of these programs, called "The National Software Guide for Nonprofit Organizations," is published annually by the publisher of *Contributions*, a monthly philanthropy newsletter. The International Catholic Stewardship Council annually publishes the results of a Software Programs Survey conducted among all dioceses in the United States and Canada. *Fund-raising Management* magazine includes a thorough overview of donor management software in one of their issues each year (see Chapter 20).

2. DONOR RECOGNITION

The two most powerful words in the fund-raiser's vocabulary, by far, are "Thank You." Nothing reinforces a donor's philanthropic intent more than manifestations of gratitude for his or her kindness. Curiously, however, one of the worrisome topics on many charitable organization's fund-raising agenda is the issue of donor recognition. Every professional fund-raiser has a collection of personal horror stories about donors who received an expression of gratitude, or some form of acknowledgment of a gift, which precipitated a scathing letter or blistering phone call from the donors about the organization "wasting time and money to thank them!" Nonetheless, the vast majority of donors need and appreciate some form of acknowledgment of their gifts.

Donor recognition in a parish setting—particularly a total-stewardship parish—can be problematic. The intent of parish stewardship conversion is to promote a stewardship way of life among all parishioners. Thanking or singling out individual members for recognition may seem redundant and even counterproductive. Yet everyone needs heroes—those people whose personal devotion and dedication inspire and encourage others to greater accomplishments and deeper commitments. A carefully crafted recognition program, even in a total-stewardship parish, can help to invigorate a parish community.

Donor recognition can take many forms: memorials, naming a building or other object, plaques, gratitude dinners, publishing names in publications, token gifts, and so on. Occasionally a parishioner will explicitly request that no receipt or acknowledgment for a gift be sent and/or that the gift should be anonymous. In these cases, it's still recommended that the pastor discreetly acknowledge the gift and express his gratitude when he speaks privately with the donor at a parish function or elsewhere. A handshake and a kind word of thanks still work wonders even with enigmatic donors.

3. SPENDING MONEY TO RAISE MONEY

Another fund-raising subject that often generates strong feelings and heated discussions is the practice of spending money to raise money. Parishes and other nonprofit organizations are forever grappling with such questions as (1) should we hire a professional fund-raising consultant; (2) should we print a slick, four-color case statement brochure; (3) should we hold a fancy special events fund-raising dinner?

Unfortunately, there's no handy rule-of-thumb to guide parish leaders through this potential human meteor shower. A parish must know its members well enough to make intelligent decisions regarding this issue. When the topic must be addressed, it might be helpful to solicit feedback from a random sampling of parishioners. However, their input could cause an unwanted backlash. Too often, overcautious leaders are driven to make decisions based on opinions expressed by small, vocal minorities rather than from the will of the entire community.

Experienced leaders know that every decision generates its share of supporters and critics—it's just human nature at work. There are some people who are dissatisfied with *any* decision, regardless of its merits; naysayers are always with us! Fortunately, for most parishes, fund-raising success or failure is generally measured by the amount of money raised and the progress achieved, not by the antics of a few immutably negative individuals!

In most cases, money spent to raise money is simply a good investment that reaps abundant dividends. Even the unhappy few will often have a change of heart when confronted with the happy results.

4. FRIEND-RAISING

Fund-raising efforts are sustained by a cluster of activities frequently referred to as "friend-raising." Friend-raising is simply a genteel euphemism for a wide variety of public relations and marketing activities that take place within a nonprofit setting. In the business community, public relations and marketing are specialized disciplines; parishes and other Catholic organizations can learn much from public relations and marketing experts.

Here, for example, is the official American Marketing Association definition of "marketing":

> Marketing is the process of planning and executing the conception, pricing, promotion, and distribution of ideas, goods, and services to create exchanges that satisfy individual and organizational objectives.

If we look beyond marketing as a "business" activity and think of it as human interaction, it's easy to see that Jesus Christ was a master marketer; one would expect nothing less from the Son of God! Let's consider each element of this definition in relationship to the mission and ministries of Catholic parishes and other Catholic organizations:

A process of planning and executing: In Chapter 19 which follows, you will find a strong case for intentional long-range planning for any organization striving for excellence. A marketing component should be incorporated into a parish's strategic plan (those who prefer ecclesiastical jargon to business jargon might choose "evangelization" instead of "marketing"). A typical marketing plan has these five components:

1. Introduction—description and analysis of the markets that are served plus an overview of the organization and its general marketing philosophy.
2. Marketing research—research results, forecasts, competition, problems, opportunities, and assumptions.
3. Action programs—marketing strategies and objectives, product/service programs, pricing, communications program, and sales/distribution procedures.
4. Financial data—budget information.
5. Summary/Appendix.

With a little ingenuity, parish leaders can adapt this marketing plan format to a parish setting and develop measurable ways to promote a parish and its stewardship way of life.

Conception, pricing, promotion, and distribution: A parish is its people and the relationships that bind them together. Parishes need to be sensitive to their "target markets" and find effective ways to strengthen relationships, improve communications, develop, promote, and deliver programs and services, and measure the cost-effectiveness of the parish's total operation.

Of ideas, goods, and services: A strategic plan must include a clear response to this question: "What business are we in?" Catholic parishes are engaged in and are identified by their programs and services. A parish committed to stewardship conversion never assumes that it has reached the highest level of the three elements that identify a total-stewardship parish: prayer, hospitality, and service.

To create exchanges that satisfy individual and organizational objectives: As a living community of faith, a parish needs to constantly assess its prayer life, the caliber of its hospitality, and the scope and quality of its programs and services. How are they communicated and measured? Are individual and organizational needs being met? Are there gaps and weaknesses?

We say it once again: the success of parish fund-raising and stewardship conversion is largely dependent on the relationship that parishioners have with their parish. Friend-raising activities—the cultivation of donors and parishioners through effective marketing and public relations—form the foundation upon which stewardship of treasure is constructed.

5. GOVERNANCE

In the United States, a parish is technically a nonprofit organization. However, when issues of oversight and decision-making arise within a parish setting, the customary formula for nonprofit governance—a board of directors, an executive director, relevant committees—doesn't quite fit. In the Catholic Church, the pastor is to his parish somewhat as a bishop is to his diocese. He's not only the boss, his final word is, in certain instances, the *final* word. Official parish leadership groups, such as a parish council or finance committee are only consultative. (See Chapter 11 for more information about this and related issues.)

With these observations in mind, let's review the usual characteristics, attributes, and other pertinent issues which relate to "normal" nonprofit boards of directors.

Role of the Board: Duties and responsibilities of board members can be summarized under these headings:

- *Active participation:* Members are expected to attend board meetings and serve on at least one of the board's committees.
- *Provide direction:* The board determines policies and creates long-range plans.
- *Hire/supervise executive director:* The board hires and evaluates the work of the organization's executive director who, in turn, hires, supervises, and evaluates the work of any other staff members.
- *Perpetuate itself:* The board systematically seeks to improve itself and ensure the future of the organization by selecting and orienting committed, talented people to serve as board members.
- *Public relations:* Board members are ambassadors for the organization and share a joint obligation to promote the organization's programs and services.
- *Budget and finance:* The board is responsible for the organization's financial health which includes fund-raising, and approving and overseeing the organization's annual budget.
- *Corporate entity:* The board is responsible for maintaining the integrity of the organization's legal and incorporated status.

The three W's: Consultants for nonprofit organizations generally suggest that ideal board members should possess three attributes: wealth, wisdom, and work. "Wealth" encompasses not only personal financial resources but also a substantial measure of influence, both of which can be employed to raise funds and generate support for the organization. "Wisdom" and "work" refer to the personal gifts of time, energy, and specialized talents and skills that each board member contributes to the organization.

Selection or election? Choosing good board members is both an art and a science. As a science, board selection is greatly facilitated by written job descriptions that tell prospective board members exactly what is expected of them, and remind current board members about the kind of people they are looking for to perpetuate their work. As an art, board selection is (1) finding a "match" between a board's leadership needs and a prospective member's gifts and talents; and (2) the interpersonal skills necessary to cultivate prospective members.

Performance evaluation: An often-overlooked aspect of organizational governance is the need for performance evaluations both by and for board members. This is obviously a sensitive issue for nonprofit organizations since their board members are typically volunteers who serve without remuneration, and their staff members are motivated more by altruistic motives than by large salaries and benefit packages. Nonetheless, it's eminently wise for nonprofit boards to conduct periodic self-evaluations and assessments of the agencies they serve; it's equally advisable for board members themselves to be evaluated regarding their performance as board members. The National Center for Nonprofit Boards maintains an extensive catalogue of publications and assessment instruments designed to help boards improve themselves and the operation of their organizations. (See Chapter 20 for further references and resources.)

The QBQ: The "Quickie Board Quiz" is a checklist designed to give an organization's leaders an immediate global assessment of the elements necessary for efficient and effective operation. For this quiz, see Appendix 9.

6. CATHOLIC SCHOOL TUITION: ANOTHER LOOK

In Chapter 11, we explained the official IRS rulings regarding the tax-deductibility of Catholic school tuition. In general, tuition paid for private school education is not tax deductible. There are, however, two additional topics regarding Catholic school tuition which must be considered within the context of fund-raising and stewardship of treasure: (1) parish support; and (2) tithing.

Tuition and parish support: In many cases, Catholic school tuition cannot legitimately be viewed as parish support. This is particularly true if the tuition is for an elementary school in a parish which also has a financial obligation for its parishioner-students who attend a Catholic high school. Catholic school tuition generally does not cover the total annual cost of educating each child. The difference between tuition payments and actual cost is frequently covered by special fund-raising activities and additional parish subsidies. Parents whose tuition payments constitute their total contributions to a parish are frequently contributing nothing to the support of parish programs and services beyond simply providing a Catholic education for their children.

Tuition and tithing: Can tuition payments for Catholic education be considered part of one's tithe? A parishioner recently heard a visiting missionary say this about Christian tithing: "You can legitimately include your annual federal and state tax payments in your tithing calculations. Why? Because both the state and federal governments spend a significant portion of your taxes for social welfare programs to help the poor and needy." This is truly a creative idea, but hardly in keeping with the intent of the biblical mandate to return at least 10 percent of one's "first fruits."

But what about tuition paid to a Catholic school? Can this legitimately be included in the calculation of one's tithe or proportional giving? Here are a few of the salient points which converge around this issue.

- Parents who pay Catholic school tuition are receiving something in return: an education for their children.
- These same parents also support public education through their taxes.
- Catholic schools are a vital source of leadership for the U.S. Catholic Church and they provide healthy competition that tends to improve the quality of all education where public and private educational systems exist side by side.
- Catholic education is rooted in the type of faith tradition and strong values that the Founding Fathers intended as the basis for government and social conduct in the United States.
- When parents no longer must pay Catholic school tuition, their level of support for their parish and Catholic school tends to decrease dramatically.

Cogent, compelling arguments can be made for both sides of the question about Catholic school tuition as part of one's tithe. Ultimately, Catholic school parents must prayerfully and honestly decide for themselves whether what they pay as tuition is truly a generous return to God in gratitude for the gifts and blessings God has bestowed upon them.

7. DO-IT-YOURSELF OR HIRE A PRO?

In Chapter 12, under the discussion of capital campaigns, we raised the issue of hiring outside fund-raising consultants. Here's an expanded look at some of the principal topics which impact this decision.

Does your parish really need outside help? Most of the actual work of capital fund-raising will be conducted by your parish staff members and volunteers. Is what a professional fund-raising company wants you to purchase something your parish is capable of accomplishing on its own? Many diocesan stewardship and development offices can provide the guidance and training parishes need for capital campaigns or other fund-raising efforts. For most capital campaigns in most parishes, hiring outside fund-raising counsel is neither necessary nor cost-efficient, and it certainly won't guarantee a campaign's success.

Fund-raising consultants are eager to sell their services: When a parish solicits proposals from professional fund-raising consultants, the resulting interactions take place on a "salesperson-customer" level. Reputable fund-raising companies sincerely want to help your parish raise the money it needs, but they are also intent on convincing you to buy their services, and usually with a hefty price tag.

At every point of the selection process, remember that the parish is the customer. Your parish is considering paying a substantial sum of money to total strangers in hopes of reaching a fund-raising goal. It's neither rude nor impolite to pose tough, legitimate questions which will help your selection committee make the best possible decision. Here are a few sample issues to raise with professional fund-raising companies.

- How conversant is the company with the latest fund-raising technology?
- Is the company able to "read" the nature of your organization quickly and even seem to intuitively anticipate issues and concerns before they arise?
- What about references? Are they current and fully disclosed? (Check references thoroughly; don't rely solely on the company's representatives.)
- What is the company's style and ability when it comes to solving problems?

- Ask prospective consultants to tell you about the most recent unsuccessful campaigns they directed. What happened?
- What are the qualifications of the company's staff members in their home office? What about the track record of the person who would be assigned to your campaign (see "halo-effect" below), and what kind of support and supervision would he or she receive from the company?
- What is the company's fee-structure? Are there any hidden costs? (NOTE: Consulting fees based on a percentage of funds raised are considered by most professional fund-raisers to be inappropriate, if not unethical.)

Beware of the "halo-effect": When presenting their services for consideration, some fund-raising consulting companies employ a version of the "halo-effect" (some have also referred to this tactic as "bait-and-switch"). It works like this: the company's top person or premier sales team comes to meet with an organization's selection committee to pitch their programs and services. The committee is understandably impressed and leans heavily in favor of choosing the company to direct the organization's capital campaign. There's just one hitch: the person who will be assigned by the company to direct the campaign is often not the person or persons who so profoundly impressed the search committee. Here's where an organization must be quite circumspect in its decision to engage one consulting company instead of another.

The success of a capital campaign will hinge greatly on the caliber of person the company assigns to direct the campaign. If a campaign falls short because of an inadequate director, many nonprofit organizations tend to accept the failure because of the lingering halo-effect created by the classy presentation that "sold" the company in the first place. The negative repercussions of a halo effect can be greatly reduced or eliminated simply by including the actual campaign director in the decision-making process. The organization's search committee should meet with and interview the consulting company's employee who will be assigned to direct the campaign, and also ask for a history of his or her track record and references. An organization wants a campaign director who is a good "fit." He or she should possess a temperament and personal qualities that match well with the organization's staff and volunteers, be able to quickly assess the characteristics of the donor-universe, and be passionately committed to the project.

Don't minimize the importance of a competent feasibility study: A feasibility study usually consists of a series of interviews with top leaders associated with an organization, and is designed to assess the potential for the organization to successfully conduct a major capital campaign. If done well, a feasibility study will not only provide the organization with a realistic approximation of the campaign goal, it will also produce a group of donors who have already indicated a level of personal commitment to the campaign.

Some companies that conduct feasibility studies occasionally engage in high-balling or low-balling the results. High-balling refers to reporting to a client-organization's leaders that their fund-raising goal is achievable, even when the study's results indicate that the desired goal is much too ambitious (in other words, telling the customers what they want to hear, not necessarily the facts). This practice often takes place when a company has been hired to direct a campaign for a specific period of time (two months, three months, and so on). When time runs out for the company's campaign director, he or she will issue a final report to the organization and move on to his or her next assignment, regardless of the status of the campaign. The organization is still obligated to pay the contracted fee.

Low-balling can happen when a fund-raising company has been engaged to conduct a capital campaign for an organization that does not have a specific goal in mind. The fund-raising goal recommended by the consultant is substantially lower than the potential goal determined by the consultant's feasibility study. This practice is sometimes employed when a fund-raising firm has been hired to help an organization create and direct a new or struggling annual fund drive. The fund-raising company wants to ensure that it will be lauded for its success and possibly be invited back to manage the annual campaign for one or two additional years before turning the campaign over to the organization's development office.

An organization can reduce the possibility of a fund-raising company using either of these practices by asking to see the results of the company's five or ten most recent feasibility studies and the campaigns which followed them.

Cost should not be the primary consideration: Fund-raising consulting services are not inexpensive. Consequently, many organizations tend to base their selection of fund-raising counsel mostly on price. Remember, however, that the expense of hiring fund-raising help is an investment in the success of a major capital campaign. Much more important than a company's price tag is its track record and ability to work effectively with diverse organizations. It may be wiser, for example, to give more weight to companies which specialize in capital fund-raising rather those whose fund-raising scope tends to be more general. We repeat: cost, although important, should not be the principal determining factor in making a final selection among several fund-raising consultants.

In the final analysis, when selecting fund-raising counsel, caveat emptor applies!

PART 3

THE BIG PICTURE

CHAPTER 18

The Parish As Steward

Total-parish stewardship can be achieved only if each parishioner truly believes "this is my parish; I own it and am responsible for its vitality and future." We would be remiss, however, if we didn't point out that such aggressive parish ownership carries a risk of excessive parochialism.

Parochialism is a "churchy" word for an attitude that says, "No matter what, I will protect and defend my parish at all costs, even if other parishes and my diocese must suffer." Parochialism is committed-Catholicism gone awry and is based on a misguided ecclesiology. In the extreme, it's a "my-parish-right-or-wrong" mentality which is contrary to the gospel message and the common good of the entire Christian community.

In its worst manifestation, parochialism pits parish against diocese, and/or parish against other parishes. This malady becomes particularly evident when a diocese must face the painful reality that some parishes must be discontinued. In these increasingly common instances, people who proclaim themselves to be good Christians sometimes exhibit terribly unchristian behavior in their refusal to face objective inevitability.

Total-parish stewardship, in its ideal form, produces a reasonable, Christ-centered balance between "what is good for my parish, and what is best for all of the people of God." The negative influences of parochialism cannot gain a foothold when parishioners' lifestyles and attitudes reflect the knowledge that we own nothing; everything we have belongs to God, the source of all our blessings. "My parish" is really "God's people gathered." *Where* God's people congregate is of no particular consequence because, as we know, where two or three are gathered, Christ is in their midst.

Parishes and dioceses throughout the United States are engaging in heroic stewardship initiatives which mitigate against the destructive effects of parochialism. One such initiative is the practice of tithing or proportionate giving by parishes and entire dioceses. A portion of parish or diocesan income is "tithed" or proportionately set aside for worthy charitable uses and/or as a replacement alternative for annual special collections.

Other such initiatives involve affluent parishes financially "adopting" struggling parishes, or the practice of parish "twinning" or "clustering" by which two or more parishes join forces and pool their unique strengths and resources, such as income, management, personnel, equipment, facilities, and so on.

Sadly, much of the impetus for these creative interparochial and intradiocesan ventures is fueled by a clergy shortage crisis which is currently gripping many dioceses. It would be eminently more Christian, of course, if such activities originated from a commitment to total stewardship. Nevertheless, these and similar endeavors provide solid evidence that stewardship conversion is indeed gaining a foothold throughout the United States. Furthermore, a parish or a diocese which operates as a corporate good steward serves as an excellent stewardship model and motivator for its members.

CHAPTER 19

The Critical Role Of Planning

The plans of the diligent lead surely to abundance.

Proverbs 21:5

"Would you tell me, please, which way I ought to go from here?" said Alice.

"That depends a good deal on where you want to get to," said the Cat.

"I don't much care where...," said Alice.

"Then it doesn't matter which way you go," said the Cat.

Lewis Carroll, Alice in Wonderland

If you fail to plan, you plan to fail.

Business Axiom

When the Catholic Church was just a handful of apostles and disciples traveling the countryside spreading the Good News of Jesus Christ, things were pretty simple. The memories of Jesus and his words were deeply etched in their minds and hearts. Most of them had experienced his magnificent presence. They had witnessed the wonders. They had agonized over his death and rejoiced in his resurrection. And they had received a massive dose of the Holy Spirit that filled them with almost superhuman courage and endurance.

But that was two millennia ago. The original mustard seed has become a forest! The Catholic Church is now an enormously diverse and complex organization. Each country, each diocese, and, indeed, each parish has a unique corporate personality which has evolved over many centuries. Fundamental Catholic dogmas, rooted in Scripture and Tradition, remain unchanged and are shared by all, almost miraculously. But the manner in which they are transmitted and the style by which they are lived can be found in a panoply of variations throughout the world.

During the years immediately following the Second Vatican Council, local churches grappled with implementation of the Council documents. Some communities, indeed, some entire countries struggled more than others. During those years, for example, some western European theologians noted that the U.S. Catholic Church was having greater difficulty than many other countries coping with Vatican II fallout. European Catholics did not share the same rigid, letter-of-the-law attitude about nonessential elements of the Catholic faith tradition that was characteristic of most American Catholics.

But today's Church is different from yesterday's; tomorrow's Church will be different still. The concept of change can no longer be treated as a leisurely, almost imperceptible evolutionary transformation. The perception of change in today's world is represented by the mind-boggling speed of the latest computer chip.

In a society that is so profoundly impacted by exponential change, each community, each organization, each parish must make a choice: either allow change to manipulate its endeavors and control its mission, or take charge of its destiny and set its own direction and priorities. If parishes and dioceses choose to take control of their futures, they must utilize some form of strategic, long-range planning.

1. THE VALUE OF PLANNING

For some Alices in Wonderland, planning has negative connotations. It evokes images of interminable meetings, small-group sharing, sheet after sheet of newsprint taped to meeting-room walls, and voluminous long-range plans that are shoved into huge, three-ring binders, distributed to everyone who can handle their weight, and quickly placed on a bookshelf never again to be consulted. The fact is, some long-range planning processes are poorly conceived, inadequately conducted, and their results are promptly—and perhaps rightly—dismissed.

Efficacious planning does not make an organization's present and future operations and activities more complicated and difficult, it makes them simpler and easier: easier to understand, easier to measure (and therefore to celebrate), easier to make adjustments along the way, easier to communicate with long-timers and newcomers, and easier to create ownership among key stakeholders. A good parish plan makes it easier to evangelize, easier to coax strays back to the fold, easier to assess parish strengths and weaknesses, easier to rejoice in the former and remediate the latter. Planning gives a community freedom to dream about what can be, and blanket permission to pursue that dream.

2. THE ELEMENTS OF PLANNING

There are a multitude of effective planning models, none of which can be called the "right" or "best way" to plan. There are, however, certain common elements in most effective planning processes. Here are a few.

- *Top-to-bottom commitment to the process.* Planning works when everyone involved unconditionally owns the process, and all the resources needed for its successful completion are provided.
- *Designated process director.* Someone must be responsible for organizing and administering the planning process. That person may be a staff member or a committed, responsible volunteer. He or she takes care of all the details so that the process can unfold in an orderly and effective manner. He or she manages every stage of the process: initial feedback/research, scheduling, progress reporting, completion, and evaluation.
- *Vision and mission statements.* Good planning begins at the beginning: with a clear statement of "who we are" (the mission) and "where we are going" (the vision).
- *Process schedule of events.* Planning takes time and focused energy. Those involved in the process should know at the outset what will be required of them and adjust their schedules accordingly.
- *Knowledgeable, skilled facilitator.* Conducting a strategic planning process requires specialized knowledge and advanced group dynamics skills. With a little research, most parishes can access professional planning assistance through diocesan offices or from corporations, universities, or private consultants in their region.
- *Market survey/needs assessment.* In order to set a direction, it's

necessary to know the starting point. It's also necessary to engage everyone who will ultimately benefit from the plan in the process. A well-designed survey and needs-assessment instrument can produce both results.

- *Realistic, measurable goals and objectives.* When the plan is completed, it must be workable, and its goals must be observable and achievable.
- *Follow-through strategies.* A strategic plan should be a living document, not a static one. Movement toward a plan's goals and objectives should be deliberate, even relentless. Goals and objectives should be accompanied by the names of those who are responsible for driving them to their destination. A system of monitoring and reporting progress should be attached. Adjustments may be made along the way as required.

3. ASKING THE RIGHT QUESTIONS: THE PARISH SURVEY

Why do some organizations fail while others flourish? There are as many answers to this question as there are successful and failed organizations. There is, however, one response that may apply in every case: not understanding the difference between "doing the job right" and "doing the right job."

When people work, either in their homes or elsewhere, they usually work hard. They are generally conscientious, reliable, and dedicated to their chosen or assigned tasks. But "working hard" does not always guarantee personal or professional success. It's entirely possible for someone to do a job right, that is, work hard, but the job they are doing may not be the right job! They may be filling a need that doesn't exist, or creating a product or providing a service that nobody wants.

Likewise, some planning processes are dismal failures while others are gloriously successful. What makes the difference? In many cases success or failure can be traced back to the fundamental planning process questions; they may have been answered correctly, but were they the correct questions? Effective planning hinges on asking—and answering—the right questions.

Here are sample sentence stems that might be included in a needs assessment/survey instrument to help jumpstart the planning process.

- The things I like most about our parish are…
- The things I like least about our parish are…
- I wish our parish would…
- I wish our parish would not…
- Our parish needs…
- Our parish should…
- I think our parish…

Here are examples of questions that can generate input for developing an organization's mission and vision statements:

- What is our parish's business?
- Whom does our parish serve?
- What does our parish do best?
- What outcomes/results does our parish desire?
- What is special about our parish and the way it operates?
- What if our parish didn't exist?
- Complete these sentences:
  (1) Our parish is…
  (2) The mission or purpose of our parish is…
  (3) Our parish longs to be…

Here are sample questions designed to elicit raw data which can be used to formulate organizational goals and objectives:

- What are our parish weaknesses and liabilities in terms of each of the following:
  (1) a caring people?
  (2) a business enterprise?
  (3) a worshiping community?
- What do you think about a direction for our parish?
  (1) What should we be?
  (2) What programs and services should we provide?
  (3) What needs should we be meeting?
- What does our parish need to make its future a reality?
  (1) What programs and services?
  (2) What facilities and equipment?
  (3) What human resources and personnel?

- What are the five biggest problems our parish will face in the next ten years?
- What should our parish do to start its move into the next decade? immediately? long-range?
- Given unlimited resources, what would our ideal parish look like?
- What does our parish need to continue/improve?
- What does our parish need to finish/complete?
- What does our parish need to start/initiate?

CHAPTER 20

References And Resources

The stewardship-conversion movement in the U.S. Catholic Church has moved out of its childhood into young adulthood. As it continues to gain momentum and mature, quality stewardship-related educational and promotional materials are increasingly easy to find. Many dioceses and parishes are actively engaged in developing and refining their own stewardship renewal-processes and resource materials. Several exchange programs, administered through the International Catholic Stewardship Council, provide excellent vehicles for tapping into the wealth of superb stewardship programs currently being created within the U.S. Catholic Church. In addition, consulting firms that specialize in Catholic fund-raising are scrambling to produce their unique brands of parish stewardship programs to promote to prospective clients.

Fund-raising, unlike the youthful stewardship movement, is a highly developed professional discipline with a long, proud history. Consequently, outstanding fund-raising resources and educational materials have been quite plentiful for many years. On the following pages, you will find a list of many of the premier resources and reference works for serious students of both stewardship conversion and fund-raising. For additional related books and articles, please refer to the Bibliography.

1. STEWARDSHIP RESOURCES

A. National Organizations

1. Center for Applied Research in the Apostolate (CARA)
   Georgetown University
   Washington, DC 20057-1203
   Phone: (202) 687-8080
   Fax: (202) 687-8083
   E-mail: CARA@gunet.georgetown.edu
   Web Site: www.georgetown.edu/research/CARA

2. National Catholic Conference for Total Stewardship
   1633 North Cleveland Ave.
   Chicago, IL 60614
   Phone: (773) 363-8046
   Fax: (773) 363-2123

3. International Catholic Stewardship Council, Inc. (ICSC)
   1275 K Street, NW, Suite 980
   Washington, DC 20005-4006
   Phone: (202) 289-1093
   Fax: (202) 682-9018
   E-mail: icscs@catholicstewardship.org
   Web Site: www.catholicstewardship.org

4. National Conference of Catholic Bishops (NCCB)/
   United States Catholic Conference (USCC)
   Publishing Services
   3211 Fourth Street, NE
   Washington, DC 20017-1194
   Phone: (202) 541-3000
   Web Site: www.nccbuscc.org

B. Magazines, Periodicals, and Electronic Subscription Services

1. *Joyful Noiseletter*
   Fellowship of Merry Christians
   P.O. Box 895
   Portage, MI 49081-0895
   Phone: (800) 877-2757
   Fax: (616) 324-3984
   Web Site: http://www.JOYFULNOISELETTER.COM

2. *ParishWorks* and *FaithWorks* newsletters
   Order Administration—Liguori Publications
   One Liguori Drive
   Liguori, MO 63057-9999
   Phone: (800) 325-9521
   Web Site: www.liguori.org

3. PastoraLink Electronic Subscription Service
   Liguori Publications
   One Liguori Drive
   Liguori, MO 63057-9999
   Phone: (636) 464-2500
   Web Site: www.liguori.org

4. *Resource*
   ICSC (International Catholic Stewardship Council)
   1275 K Street, NW, Suite 980
   Washington, DC 20005
   Phone: (202) 289-1093
   Fax: (202) 682-9018
   Web Site: www.catholicstewardship.org

C. Diocesan Stewardship Programs

What follows is only a partial list; see the latest ICSC stewardship exchange program for additional listings.

1. Albany, New York
2. Charlotte, North Carolina
3. Colorado Springs, Colorado
4. Covington, Kentucky
5. Evansville, Indiana
6. Grand Rapids, Michigan
7. Louisville, Kentucky
8. New Orleans, Louisiana
9. Owensboro, Kentucky
10. Philadelphia, Pennsylvania
11. Rockford, Illinois
12. St. Augustine, Florida
13. St. Louis, Missouri
14. St. Petersburg, Florida
15. Springfield, Illinois

D. Commercial Publications/Materials

1. Liguori Publications
   One Liguori Drive
   Liguori, MO 63057-9999
   Phone: (636) 464-2500
   Web Site: www.liguori.org

2. Our Sunday Visitor Press
   200 Noll Plaza
   Huntington, IN 46750
   Phone: (800) 348-2886
   Web Site: www.osv.com

3. Theological Book Service
   P.O. Box 509
   Barnhart, MO 63012
   Phone: (877) 484-1600
   Fax: (800) 325-9526
   Web Site: www.theobooks.org

2. FUND-RAISING RESOURCES

A. Fund-Raising Organizations

1. American Association of Fund-Raising Counsel
   25 West 43rd Street, Suite 820
   New York, NY 10036
   Phone: (212) 354-5799
   Fax: (212) 768-1795
   Web Site: www.AAFRC.org

2. The Fund-Raising School
   Indiana University Center on Philanthropy
   550 West North Street, Suite 301
   Indianapolis, IN 46202-3162
   Phone: (317) 236-4912
   Fax: (317) 684-8900
   Web Site: www.philanthropy.iupui.edu

3. Independent Sector
   1200 Eighteenth St. NW
   Suite 200
   Washington, DC 20036
   Phone: (202) 467-6100
   Fax: (202) 467-6101
   Web Site: www.indepsec.org

4. National Catholic Development Conference
   86 Front Street
   Hempstead, NY 11550-3667
   Phone: (516) 481-6000
   Fax: (516) 489-9287
   Web Site: www.amm.org

5. National Society of Fund-Raising Executives (NSFRE)
   1101 King Street, Suite 700
   Alexandria, VA 22314
   Phone: (703) 684-0410
   Fax: (703) 684-0540
   E-mail: nsfre@nsfre.org
   Web Site: www.nsfre.org

B. Magazines, Periodicals, and Publications

1. *The Chronicle of Philanthropy*
   1255 Twenty-Third Street, NW
   Washington, DC 20037
   Phone: (740) 382-3322

2. *Communication Briefings*
   1101 King Street
   Suite 110
   Alexandria, VA 22314
   Phone: (800) 888-2084

3. *Contributions*
   P.O. Box 338
   Medfield, MA 02052
   Phone: (508) 359-0019

4. *Corporate Philanthropy Report*
   1101 King Street, Suite 444
   Alexandria, VA 22314
   Phone: (703) 683-4100

5. *Fund-Raising Management*
   224 Seventh Street
   Garden City, NY 11530
   Phone: (516) 746-6700

6. *Giving USA*
   AAFRC Trust for Philanthropy
   25 West 43rd Street, Suite 820
   New York, NY 10036
   Phone: (212) 354-5799
   Web Site: www.AAFRC.org

7. *NonProfit Times*
   240 Cedar Knolls Road, Suite 318
   Cedar Knolls, NJ 07927-1621
   Phone: (973) 734-1700
   Fax: (973) 734-1777

8. *NonProfit World*
   6314 Odana Road, Suite 1
   Madison, WI 53719-1141
   Phone: (800) 424-7367
   Fax: (608) 274-9978
   E-mail: snpo@danenet.wicip.org
   Web Site: danenet.wicip.org/snpo

9. *The Philanthropy Monthly*
   2 Bennitt Street
   P.O. Box 989
   New Milford, CT 06776
   Phone: (203) 354-7132

C. Specialized Resources/Materials

a. Board Development

National Center for Nonprofit Boards
1828 L Street, NW, Suite 900
Washington, DC 20036-5104
Phone: (202) 452-6262
E-mail: ncnb@ncnb.org

b. Donor Rights

1. National Charities Information Bureau (NCIB)
   19 Union Square West
   New York, NY 10003-3395
   Phone: (212) 929-6300
   Fax: (212) 463-7083
   Web Site: www.give.org

2. National Committee for Responsive Philanthropy
   2001 S Street, NW, Suite 620
   Washington, DC 20009
   Phone: (202) 387-9177
   E-mail: info@ncrp.org

c. Grant Seeking

1. *The Catholic Funding Guide*
   FADICA, Inc.
   1350 Connecticut Ave., NW, Suite 303
   Washington, DC 20036-1701
   Web Site: www.fadica.org

2. Council on Foundations, Inc.
   1828 L Street, NW, Suite 300
   Washington, DC 20036
   Phone: (202) 466-6512
   Web Site: www.cof.org

3. The Foundation Center
   79 Fifth Avenue
   New York, NY 10003-3076
   Phone: (212) 620-4230
   Web Site: www.fdncenter.org

4. The Grantsmanship Center
   1125 W. Sixth Street, Fifth Floor
   P.O. Box 17220
   Los Angeles, CA 90017
   Phone: (213) 482-9860, or
   (800)421-9512
   Fax: (213) 482-9863
   Web Site: www.tgci.com

5. Lilly Endowment, Inc.
   P.O. Box 88068
   Indianapolis, IN 46208-0068
   Phone: (317) 924-5471
   Fax: (517) 926-4431

6. State foundation directories produced annually by individual state donor alliances; check with professional fund-raisers in your state.

7. Repositories of IRS 1099 tax forms for foundations in each state; these tax records are accessible in designated public libraries and other locations within each state.

d. Matching Gifts

Council for Advancement and Support of Education (CASE)
1307 New York Avenue, NW
Suite 1000
Washington, DC 20005
Phone: (202) 328-2273
E-mail: gopher.case.org
Web Site: www.case.org

e. Planned Giving/Estate Planning

1. American Council on Gift Annuities
   2401 Cedar Springs Road
   Dallas, TX 75201-1427
   Phone: (214) 720-4774
   Fax: (214) 720-2105

2. National Committee on Planned Giving
   233 McCrea Street, Suite 400
   Indianapolis, IN 46225
   Phone: (317) 269-6274
   E-mail: byeager@iupui.edu

3. ICSC planned giving exchange program
   (See also ICSC above)

4. *Planned Giving Today*
   100 Second Avenue South
   Suite 180
   Edmonds, WA 98020
   Phone: (800) 525-5748
   Fax: (425) 744-3838

f. Software/Computer Programs

Several organizations produce comprehensive annual computer software guides including:

1. "The National Software Guide for Nonprofit Organizations," published annually by *Contributions.* (See previous listing.)

2. "Planned Giving Software Vendor List" published by the American Council on Gift Annuities. (See previous listing.)

3. ICSC Arch/Diocesan Software Programs Survey (annual)

g. Status of Church Giving

1. empty tomb, inc.
   301 North Fourth Street
   P.O. Box 2404
   Champaign, IL 61825-2404
   Phone: (217) 356-9519

2. Lilly Endowment, Inc.
   P.O. Box 88068
   Indianapolis, IN 46208-0068
   Phone: (317) 924-5471
   Fax: (517) 926-4431

h. Legal Issues

Office of the General Counsel
United States Catholic Conference
3211 4th Street, N.E.
Washington, DC 20017-1194
Phone: (202) 541-3300
Fax: (202) 541-3337

i. Commercial Fund-Raising Consultants

Consult the classified ad section of the fund-raising periodicals listed above.

3. ITEMS FOR YOUR "TO-DO" LIST

- Join the International Catholic Stewardship Council.
- Put your parish on the ICSC stewardship and planned giving exchange lists.
- Encourage parishioners to pick up sample stewardship materials from parishes they visit when traveling.
- Never be satisfied with the quality and progress of your stewardship-conversion process. Constantly evaluate what you do, how you do it, the caliber of your printed materials, and so on.
- Become very friendly with the Internet. There's no end to the help you can receive for your stewardship efforts through this marvelous tool.

APPENDICES

APPENDIX 1

Stewardship-Related Scripture References

Old Testament

- Genesis 28:22—"Of all that you give me I will surely give one tenth to you."
- Exodus 23:19—"The choicest of the first fruits of your ground you shall bring into the house of the LORD your God."
- Leviticus 27:30—"All tithes from the land, whether the seed from the ground or the fruit from the tree, are the LORD's; they are holy to the LORD."
- Deuteronomy 14:22, 29—"Set apart a tithe of all the yield of your seed that is brought in yearly from the field...so that the LORD your God may bless you in all the work that you undertake."
- Deuteronomy 16:10, 16–17—"Then you shall keep the festival of weeks for the LORD your God, contributing a freewill offering in proportion to the blessing that you have received from the LORD your God....Three times a year all your males shall appear before the LORD you God at the place that he will choose: at the festival of unleavened bread, at the festival of weeks, and at the festival of booths. They shall not appear before the LORD empty-handed; all shall give as they are able, according to the blessing of the LORD your God that he has given you."

- Deuteronomy 26:1–4, 10—"When you have come into the land that the LORD your God is giving you as an inheritance to possess, and you possess it, and settle in it, you shall take some of the first of all the fruit of the ground, which you harvest from the land that the LORD your God is giving you, and you shall put it in a basket and go to the place that the LORD your God will choose as a dwelling for his name. You shall go to the priest who is in office at that time, and say to him, 'Today I declare to the LORD your God that I have come into the land that the LORD swore to our ancestors to give us.' When the priest takes the basket from your hand and sets it down before the altar of the LORD your God, you shall make this response....'Now I bring the first of the fruit of the ground that you, O LORD, have given me.'"
- 1 Chronicles 29:12–18 (David's Prayer)—"Riches and honor come from you, and you rule over all. In your hand are power and might; and it is in your hand to make great and to give strength to all. And now, our God, we give thanks to you and praise your glorious name. But who am I, and what is my people, that we should be able to make this freewill offering? For all things come from you, and of your own have we given you. For we are aliens and transients before you, as were all our ancestors; our days on the earth are like a shadow, and there is no hope. O LORD our God, all this abundance that we have provided for building you a house for your holy name comes from your hand and is all your own. I know, my God, that you search the heart, and take pleasure in uprightness; in the uprightness of my heart I have freely offered all these things, and now I have seen your people, who are present here, offering freely and joyously to you. O LORD, the God of Abraham, Isaac, and Israel, our ancestors, keep forever such purposes and thoughts in the hearts of your people, and direct their hearts toward you."
- Proverbs 3:9—"Honor the LORD with your substance / and with the first fruits of all your produce."
- Sirach 35:7–11—"For all that you offer is in fulfillment of the commandment. / The offering of the righteous enriches the altar, / and its pleasing odor rises before the Most High. / The sacrifice of the righteous is acceptable, / and it will never be forgotten. Be generous when you worship the LORD, / and do not stint the first fruits of your hands. / With every gift show a cheerful face, / and dedicate your tithe with gladness."

New Testament

- Matthew 6:21—"For where your treasure is, there your heart will be also."
- Matthew 6:24—"No one can serve two masters; for a slave will either hate the one and love the other, or be devoted to the one and despise the other. You cannot serve God and wealth."
- Matthew 10:8—"Cure the sick, raise the dead, cleanse the lepers, cast out demons. You received without payment; give without payment."
- Luke 6:38—"Give, and it will be given to you. A good measure, pressed down, shaken together, running over, will be put into your lap; for the measure you give will be the measure you get back."
- Luke 12:33–34—"Sell your possessions, and give alms. Make purses for yourselves that do not wear out, and unfailing treasure in heaven, where no thief comes near and no moth destroys. For where your treasure is, there your heart will be also."
- Luke 12:48—"From everyone to whom much has been given, much will be required; and from the one to whom much has been entrusted, even more will be demanded."
- Acts 20:35—"In all this I have given you an example that by such work as we must support the weak, remembering the words of the Lord Jesus, for he himself said, 'It is more blessed to give than to receive.'"
- Romans 12:6–8—"We have gifts that differ according to the grace given to us: prophecy, in proportion to faith; ministry, in ministering; the teacher, in teaching; the exhorter, in exhortation; the giver, in generosity; the leader, in diligence; the compassionate, in cheerfulness."
- Romans 14:12—"So then, each of us will be accountable to God."
- 1 Corinthians 4:1—"Think of us in this way, as servants of Christ and stewards of God's mysteries."
- 1 Corinthians 12:4–7—"Now there are varieties of gifts, but the same Spirit; and there are varieties of services, but the same LORD; and there are varieties of activities, but it is the same God who activates all of them in everyone. To each is given the manifestation of the Spirit for the common good."

- 1 Corinthians 16:2—"On the first day of every week, each of you is to put aside the save whatever extra you earn, so that collections need not be taken when I come."
- 2 Corinthians 8:12—"For if the eagerness is there, the gift is acceptable according to what one has—not according to what one does not have."
- 2 Corinthians 9:6–9—"The one who sows sparingly will also reap sparingly, and the one who sows bountifully will also reap bountifully. Each of you must give as you have made up your mind, not reluctantly or under compulsion, for God loves a cheerful giver. And God is able to provide you with every blessing in abundance, so that by always having enough of everything, you may share abundantly in every good work. As it is written, / 'He scatters abroad, he gives to the poor; / his righteousness endures forever.'"
- Hebrews 13:16—"Do not neglect to do good and to share what you have, for such sacrifices are pleasing to God."
- 1 Peter 4:8–11—"Above all, maintain constant love for one another, for love covers a multitude of sins. Be hospitable to one another without complaining. Like good stewards of the manifold grace of God, serve one another with whatever gift each of you has received. Whoever speaks must do so as one speaking the very words of God; whoever serves must do so with the strength that God supplies, so that God may be glorified in all things through Jesus Christ. To him belong the glory and the power forever and ever. Amen."

Parables Dealing With Money and Possessions

Matthew 13:44—The Hidden Treasure
Matthew 13:45—The Fine Pearl
Matthew 18:23–35—The Unmerciful Servant
Matthew 20:1–16—The Generous Employer
Matthew 25:14–30; Luke 19:12–27—The Talents
Matthew 25:31–45—The Sheep and Goats
Matthew 21:33; Mark 12:1–12; Luke 20:9–19—The Wicked Tenants
Matthew 24:45–51; Luke 12:42–46—The Servant Entrusted With Supervision
Luke 7:41–43—The Two Debtors

Luke 10:25–37—The Good Samaritan
Luke 11:5–8—The Friend at Midnight
Luke 12:16–21—The Rich Fool
Luke 13:6–9—The Barren Fig Tree
Luke 14:28–30—The Tower Builder
Luke 14:31–33—The King Contemplating a Campaign
Luke 15:3–7—The Lost Sheep
Luke 15:8–10—The Lost Coin
Luke 15:11–32—The Prodigal Son
Luke 18:1–8—The Unjust Judge
Luke 18:9–14—The Pharisee and the Tax Collector

APPENDIX 2

Time and Talent Renewals: Sample Materials

On the following pages, you will find sample copies of the types of activities calendars, bulletin inserts, letters from the pastor, a self-assessment flyer and a commitment card which parishes might use during their periods of Time and Talent Stewardship Renewal. (See Chapter 4 for related materials.)

Many dioceses, the International Catholic Stewardship Council, and other organizations have developed similar materials for parish renewals. (See Chapter 20 for related material.)

Sample Bulletin Insert A

(PARISH NAME)
CATHOLIC CHURCH

STEWARDSHIP RENEWAL
TIME AND TALENT

During this time of renewal, you are being asked to look at your priorities and the needs of the world and our parish. You should use this period of renewal to consider how you can share some of your God-given time and talents for God's work. What are God's gifts to you? How do you know what you can share? Where do you begin?

To be responsible stewards of time and talent, you must begin with an honest inventory of yourself. All you are comes from God. Your very life is God's gift, and the daily sustaining of your life is proof of God's continuing desire that you develop your talents and share them.

To become good stewards, you need to know yourself as God does—to take stock of your gifts. Good stewardship obliges you to take time for prayer and reflection, to assess your gifts, your time, your ordering of life priorities. This self-inventory is the beginning.

Stewardship is itself a gift from God. With the gift of faith received in baptism, you are called to become a responsible steward. In a sense, assessing your time, talent, and treasure is not an option. For a person of faith, it is part of the commitment to participate fully in the life of the Church.

This week you will receive a letter and a brochure. The brochure will help you answer the question, "What are God's gifts to me?" With the help of this instrument, take some time to assess your God-given talents. As you begin your reflections, name your gifts and thank God for them. Then ask the Holy Spirit to help you discover how to use them well, for the church and for the world.

You are gifted! Find out just how gifted you are! Discover God within you! This discovery will lead you to a renewed life for God!

STEWARDSHIP IS A DISCIPLE'S RESPONSE

Sample Bulletin Insert B

(PARISH NAME)
CATHOLIC CHURCH

STEWARDSHIP RENEWAL:
TIME AND TALENT

What's the best gift anyone ever gave you? Was it for your birthday? anniversary? graduation? Christmas? Whatever it was, it made a lasting impression on you.

Remember when you received it how you felt a flood of emotion? As you look back on that exciting moment, you now realize you were experiencing three distinct feelings simultaneously: great *pleasure* because it was such a special gift; enormous *gratitude* toward the person who gave you the gift; and an overwhelming *desire to return the favor*, that is, to do something special for the gift-giver.

At the moment you received that gift, you fully understood the meaning of Christian Stewardship.

Stewardship is

(1) Recognition of the great joy God's gifts and blessings bring you
(2) A sense of gratitude toward God for God's gifts
(3) A desire, in fact a need, to give something back to God because God has given you so much

Good stewardship is part of our baptismal responsibility as Catholic Christians. But it's also a matching of needs: our need to give of ourselves to others, and the need others have to receive gifts, blessings, and help from us. Included under "needs of others" are the volunteer programs and services of our parish.

The Stewardship Renewal of Time and Talent Offering Card (page 172) you will receive this week will give you an opportunity to review the ways you now give of your time and talents to others and, hopefully, choose to share more of yourself with your parish, your church, and your world.

Consider your gifts from God. Then give a proportionate amount back to God through (*name*) Parish.

STEWARDSHIP IS A DISCIPLE'S RESPONSE

Sample Letter From Pastor—A

(PARISH LETTERHEAD)

Date

Dear (*name of parishioner*):

This past weekend, we began a period of parish renewal of Time and Talent Stewardship. For the next few weeks you will be invited to consider the many gifts and blessings God has showered on you, to take stock of your own interests, abilities, and skills, and then to make a commitment to share some of those abilities doing God's work in our parish and beyond.

Before you make any decisions about where and how you might become more involved in (*name*) Parish, you need to look closely at yourself. What am I doing now for my parish? What am I capable of? What kind of talents and abilities do I have that would benefit my fellow parishioners and my Church?

These are the kinds of questions you can answer for yourself by carefully reading and filling out the enclosed Parish Ministry and Your Personal Self-Assessment (pages 170–171). As you assess yourself, keep two things in mind: (1) honesty, not false modesty, is most important. Don't hesitate to write down anything you do well; and (2) why not consider some interests or activities that will "stretch" you a little? What about trying some new things that you've always wanted to do but were a little fearful? Doing something that may require taking a risk can help you grow as a person and as a Christian.

Save your Personal Self-Assessment after completing it. You will need it next week to help guide your decisions regarding the programs, organizations or activities here at (*name*) Parish you may wish to participate in or join.

Finally, remember that God has promised special blessings to those who give back a portion of God's gifts. One good place to give more of ourselves is right here at (*name*) Parish.

In Christ, the Great Steward,

(Name and Signature of Pastor)

Sample Letter From Pastor—B

(PARISH LETTERHEAD)

Date

Dear (*name of parishioner*):

Here is your Time and Talent Offering Card you've been hearing about the past few weeks. Before you fill it out or put it aside for "later," I'd like you to consider a few things. The first reaction you may have when asked to "do more" is: "I'm doing all I can now" or "I have too many other commitments" or "My family needs me more" or "I'm just too busy."

Most of these concerns are about time—how much we have and how we use it. Certainly, we're not asking people to overburden themselves by doing a little more for (*name*) Parish. But I also know how rewarding it can be to be involved in parish organizations and activities. The time and talent you give to—and for—your fellow parishioners can be uplifting and refreshing, not burdensome.

How do you spend your time now? Here's an example. If you watch TV only two hours each day (which is not hard to do: one hour of news and two favorite half-hour programs), this amounts to 730 hours of television viewing per year, which is almost the same as watching TV continuously 24 hours a day for an entire month! Perhaps you could give one of two of those hours each month back to God!

Maybe your time and talent renewal this year will mean shifting the focus of your energy and attention—making some changes. Maybe you want to give a portion of your offering to activities within or outside of our parish other than those which you have chosen in the past. Don't hesitate to take a risk and try something new. You'll benefit, and so will our parish.

Finally, we are constantly reminded in the Scriptures that we need to return to God, in gratitude, some of the gifts God has given us. For us at (*name*) Parish, this means returning a portion of our time, talents, and treasure. This is the heart and soul of good stewardship. It's our challenge and our privilege as Catholic Christians. I urge you to accept the challenge, and exercise the privilege.

In Christ, the Great Steward,

(Name and Signature of Pastor)

P.S. Please complete your Time and Talent Offering Card and place it in the collection this weekend. If you need extra cards, they are available in the gathering area of the church or at the parish office. May God continue to bless your stewardship.

YEAR Stewardship of Time/Talent Renewal – 1 **MONTH**

SUNDAY	MONDAY	TUESDAY	WEDNESDAY	THURSDAY	FRIDAY	SATURDAY
						Bullet Insert #1 ——— Pulpit Announce-ment
Bulletin Insert # 1 ——— Pulpit Announce-ment						Bulletin Insert #2 ——— Pulpit Announce-ment
Bulletin Insert # 2 ——— Pulpit Announce-ment		Mail First Letter ("A") ——— Enclose Self-Assessment				Bulletin Insert #3 ——— Pulpit Announce-ment
Bulletin Insert # 3 ——— Pulpit Announce-ment						Bulletin Insert #4 ——— Stewardship Homily
Bulletin Insert # 4 ——— Stewardship Homily		Mail Second Letter ("B") ——— Enclose Offering Card & Reply Envelope				Special Collection for Offering Cards

YEAR Stewardship of Time/Talent Renewal – 2 **MONTH**

SUNDAY	MONDAY	TUESDAY	WEDNESDAY	THURSDAY	FRIDAY	SATURDAY
Special Collection for Offering Cards		Mail "Thank You For Responding" and Follow-Up Letters				Follow-Up Offering Card Collection
Follow-Up Offering Card Collection			Telephone Committee Begins Follow-Up Phone Calls			
			Telephone Committee Completes Follow-Up Phone Calls			

TIME AND TALENT SELF-ASSESSMENT

What are God's gifts to me?

Your answers to the following questions will give you a good indication of the types of parish ministries you might like, or for which you would be best suited:

1. What is my occupation, vocation, or profession? ______
2. What additional skills, talents, or interests do I have? ______
3. What are my hobbies? What do I like to do in my spare time? ______
4. What skills or talents do I have because of my hobbies? ______
5. What kinds of things have I always wanted to do but never took the time? ______
6. What kinds of skills, talents, or abilities do my friends and family members tell me I have? ______
7. What are some specific needs of my parish that I know I could help with? ______

Compare your answers to these questions with the qualities necessary for each ministry category on the next page. What do you notice about yourself? Share your thoughts with God in prayer—and listen to what God wants you to do. Then respond generously through your Time and Talent Commitment Card during the week of (*date*).

(NAME) PARISH

TIME & TALENT STEWARDSHIP RENEWAL

PARISH MINISTRY AND YOUR PERSONAL SELF-ASSESSMENT

"This is how all will know you are my disciples: Your love for one another" (John 13:35).

STEWARDSHIP: A Disciple's Response

THE MEANING OF STEWARDSHIP

All of our gifts and blessings come from God. Stewardship is the wise and faithful use of our God-given gifts and blessings. As "stewards" we have an obligation to manage them well, and to return a just portion to help build God's kingdom on earth.

We have been called to stewardship through our baptism. Stewardship is not an option for us as Catholic Christians; it should be our way of life. The goal of our stewardship is our own salvation. We will achieve our goal only if we use our gifts and talents wisely and well.

GOD'S GIFTS TO US:
Time — Talent — Treasure
Our Return to God:
OUR STEWARDSHIP OF…
…TIME: *volunteering to serve*
…TALENTS: *using God's gifts well*
…TREASURE: *sharing the goods of the earth*

Our parish is now conducting a Time and Talent Stewardship Renewal. During these weeks we are being asked to look at our own priorities and the needs of our parish. We should use this period of renewal to consider how we can share some of our God-given time and talents for his work and to help our brothers and sisters.

REMEMBER: WE ARE OUR PARISH, YOU AND I! Our parish is an extension of our homes and families. Just like our families, it works best when all of us are involved.

Our parish brings each of us many benefits. If we truly cherish these benefits and want our parish to thrive, we must all share in the work and ministry of our Church!

WHAT IS MINISTRY

Ministry is any activity or service for our parish, its organizations and people, which helps our Church reach its goals by doing the work of Jesus. Being a good steward means participating in one or more of the ministries available in our parish. In God's eyes every ministry is important because it benefits our Church and moves us closer to our personal salvation.

THREE CATEGORIES OF MINISTRIES:

Liturgical Ministries — worship, prayer, etc.
Educational Ministries — learning, teaching, etc.
Service Ministries — helping, organizing, fixing, etc.

Each type of ministry offers interesting, unique opportunities for all members of our parish to become involved. Now is the time to review your parish stewardship of time and talent and choose the ministry or ministries which "fit" you best!

WHICH MINISTRY(IES) SHOULD I CHOOSE?

Step 1: Fill out the "Time and Talent Self-Assessment" form. Be honest! This is no time for false modesty! If you know you're good at something, admit it!

Step 2: Review the descriptions of the three ministry categories below. Compare them to your "self-assessment." Look for the best "fit." If you are interested in or suited for more than one category, ask yourself which category would be your first choice.

Step 3: Keep your choice(s) in mind until you receive your "Time and Talent Commitment Card" during the week of (*date*). You will then be asked to choose specific ministries.

REMEMBER: When you ask to be considered for specific ministries you are not volunteering for life! You are simply saying that at the present time you are willing to participate in one or more of the ministries of your choice as long as you are able and believe you have something to offer.

Here are the types of persons (talents, skills, interests) who would probably be "at home" in each of the three ministry categories:

1. **Liturgical Minister:**
   General: loves prayer and celebration; happy in gatherings of people; committed to community worship; likes positive, uplifting church celebrations and preparing feasts and seasons; wants to hear, spread, and live the Word of God.
   Specific: good "people" skills; sometimes willing to be "in the public eye"; artistic talents and skills (music, art, etc.); pleasant voice; sensitive, reflective, thoughtful.
2. **Educational Minister:**
   General: likes to explore and help others explore God's word in all facets of our lives and make it the foundation of all we are and do; believes that in knowledge there is strength; personally excited about the spiritual, physical, and mental growth of others; desires to share knowledge, experiences, and skills with others; likes to discuss issues; committed to quality parish programs and services.
   Specific: good "people" person; willing and able to share knowledge; good Christian role model; strong in faith; knows some Scripture; communicates and writes well.
3. **Service Minister:**
   General: likes to make "things" and organizations work; supports parish activities and organizations; willing to work with and support others to achieve common parish goals; good "team" player; a "do-er" rather than just an observer.
   Specific: technical skills and abilities; craftsman; good with "things"; talented in some special area of parish need; "fix-er-up-er"; willing to tackle just about anything.

My PARISH and My STEWARDSHIP

What Is the Connection?

Our parish is an extension of our homes. It is the physical and visible focal point of our faith. It is the challenge by which God gives us special graces through the sacraments. It is the public forum where we gather as a Christian community to give witness to Jesus.

Our parish gives us so much: the eucharistic celebration, the initiation of baptism and confirmation, the soothing and strengthening help of penance, the blessing of matrimony, the comfort of the sacrament of the sick, the "belonging" of community, and the security and assurance of knowing we are a people favored by God.

These wonderful benefits elicit a responsibility from each of us toward our parish as an active, living, sustaining institution. We fulfill this obligation by giving of our *time* and *talents,* and by our adequate financial support—our *treasure.*

This giving of our time, talents, and treasure to our parish constitutes our stewardship. God has blessed us greatly. In gratitude and in faith we, as good stewards, return a portion of these blessings to further God's work in our parish. *And we prayerfully strive to make stewardship not just a word, but our way of life as believing Christian Catholics.*

(Parish Name) Catholic Church

Stewardship Renewal

Time and Talent Offering Card

In recognition of…
…my need to give, and
…the many needs of my
church and parish,
and in gratitude for God's gifts to me,
I declare my willingness to return a
portion of my God-given
time,
talents,
and abilities
as part of my total
Christian stewardship.

Your signature here:

____

❑ Check here if you are unable to become more involved at this time.

PLEASE PRINT

Name ______________________

Address ______________________

City/ZIP ______________________

Home Phone: ______________________

Business Phone: ______________________

I am currently active or involved in the following parish organization(s) or ministry(ies), or other church, community, or civic organizations:

____

____

INSTRUCTIONS:

First: complete your "Self-Assessment" of your interests and abilities (see earlier brochure). *Next:* study the types of ministries available in our parish. *Finally:* choose **at least three (3) but not more than five (5)** of the ministries printed below. Put an "X" in the box provided.

Note: You will **not** *be expected to become involved in all of your choices. Within a few days you will be contacted about* **one** *of your choices (where you are needed most). At that time you will be asked about your additional choices. You are not making a commitment for life, but for as long as both you and the parish benefit from your services. Thank you.*

In fulfillment of my stewardship, I ask to be considered for the following ministries at (*parish name*) Church:

Liturgical Ministries

- ❑ artist/artisan
- ❑ choir/cantor
- ❑ communion minister
- ❑ decorator
- ❑ greeter
- ❑ lector/reader
- ❑ musician
  - instrument ______
- ❑ prayer chain
- ❑ prayer group
- ❑ sanctuary cleaner
- ❑ server
- ❑ other ______

Educational Ministries

- ❑ arts/crafts teacher
- ❑ bulletin preparer
- ❑ catechist
- ❑ graphic artist
- ❑ chaperon
- ❑ office helper/typist
- ❑ preschool teacher/aide
- ❑ religious ed. committee
- ❑ religious education
- ❑ elementary
- ❑ high school
- ❑ school board
- ❑ scouting leader
- ❑ scripture study group
- ❑ sports/coach
- ❑ stewardship committee
- ❑ teacher
- ❑ teacher aide
- ❑ tutor
- ❑ worship sheet preparer

Service Ministries

- ❑ baby-sitter
- ❑ budget/finance committee
- ❑ burgoo worker
- ❑ census worker
- ❑ CPC worker
- ❑ craftsman/woman
  - ❑ lawn care
  - ❑ carpenter
  - ❑ electrician
  - ❑ painter
  - ❑ plumber
  - ❑ mason
  - ❑ electronics
  - ❑ seamstress
  - ❑ other(s) ______
- ❑ computer expert
- ❑ estate planner
- ❑ fund-raiser
  - ❑ Fall Festival
  - ❑ lottery
- ❑ kitchen worker/cook
- ❑ Legion of Mary
- ❑ men's club
- ❑ office helper/typist
- ❑ parish council
- ❑ St. Vincent de Paul
- ❑ sewing/quilter
- ❑ social concerns/consumer interests committee
- ❑ special events organizer
- ❑ summer social
- ❑ transporter/driver
- ❑ welcomer/home visitor
- ❑ women's club
- ❑ work with elderly
- ❑ youth work
  - ❑ junior high
  - ❑ high school

APPENDIX 3

Treasure Renewals: Sample Materials

On the following pages, you will find sample copies of the types of activities calendars, bulletin inserts, letters from the pastor, and an intent card which parishes might use during their periods of Treasure Stewardship Renewal. (See Chapter 13 for related material.)

Many dioceses, the International Catholic Stewardship Council, and other organizations have developed similar materials for parish renewals. (See Chapter 20 for related material.)

Sample Bulletin Insert A

(PARISH NAME)
CATHOLIC CHURCH

STEWARDSHIP RENEWAL: TREASURE

It was almost (one year, two years, or so on) ago that our parish began the process we call Stewardship Conversion. From the very beginning it was no ordinary undertaking. It was destined to change the very way we operate as a parish. It would change the way each of us relates to God.

We have always given of ourselves, and share what we have received—sometimes generously, sometimes even heroically. But in reflecting together, we are being led to choose giving that is consistent, sacrificial, and based on faith. In a word, it is a plan of life consciously chosen; it is God's plan. We have chosen as our personal and parish ideal the way that is called Christian stewardship. That means returning to God in thanksgiving a portion of what we have received. Stewardship teaches us to receive graciously and to respond joyfully.

As individuals and as a parish we have always helped others in need. Now we recognize a need just as fundamental as the need of neighbor or church. It is the need God has placed in me to share what I am and what I have—a need recognized and fulfilled in faith. Faith gives me access to the God who is the source of everything I have and everything I will ever need.

Now it is time to rededicate ourselves with the same faith and trust with which we began. We have an opportunity to reclaim the peace that comes from serving the Lord wholeheartedly. Stewardship is never to be feared. It is a grateful and joyous response to a good God who never asks more than we can do nor wants anything but our happiness.

"Each one should give, then, as he has decided, not with regret or out of a sense of duty; for God loves the one who gives gladly. And God is able to give you more than you need, so that you will always have all you need for yourselves and more than enough for every good cause" (2 Cor 9:7–8).

STEWARDSHIP IS A DISCIPLE'S RESPONSE

Sample Bulletin Insert B

(PARISH NAME)
CATHOLIC CHURCH

STEWARDSHIP RENEWAL: TREASURE

There's an exercise sometimes used to test a person's level of trust. It's called a "trust fall" and works like this: you stand with your back to someone you think you trust—usually a friend or relative. On a signal from the person behind you, you place your feet together, stiffen your back and, without moving your feet or trying to catch yourself, you fall backwards, trusting that the person behind you will catch you before you hit the ground and injure yourself.

Choosing to practice good stewardship is a spiritual trust fall; some would call it a "leap of faith." Many questions and concerns may arise in your mind as you are now reviewing your Stewardship of Treasure: "What are my present needs and priorities?" "Should I increase my financial giving to my parish?" "Can I afford to give more?" "What about tithing—can I move close to, or even reach, the scriptural goal of giving 10 percent of my income back to God?"

If we try to answer these questions within the context of philanthropy, which refers to charitable acts and gifts, we will probably encounter great difficulty. Stewardship is not primarily about concern for others or charitable contributions. It is about faith and trust in God from which our generosity toward others flows. The basic stewardship question is not: "How much should I give?" but "How strong is my faith?"

As Christians, we believe everything we have comes from God, even life itself. In that beautiful but difficult passage from Matthew's Gospel (6:25–34) where Jesus speaks of his Father taking care of the birds and flowers, he exhorts us to place our lives in God's hands and to rid ourselves of all worries about "things."

As you renew your stewardship of treasure during these days, take a minute to read that passage from Matthew. Concentrate particularly on the last two sentences: "*So do not worry about tomorrow: for tomorrow will bring worries of its own. Today's trouble is enough for today.*" Let yourself fall into God's loving embrace. Trust that God will "catch" you—and will not let you down.

STEWARDSHIP IS A DISCIPLE'S RESPONSE

Sample Letter From Pastor—A

(PARISH LETTERHEAD)

Date

Dear (*name of parishioner*):

At all Masses last weekend, we announced the beginning of our parish Stewardship of Treasure Renewal. This is not a new program; it is part of our continuing stewardship conversion. It is not a fund drive. Rather, we are asking for your continued commitment to the principles of good stewardship by renewing your faith in the Lord and his goodness, and your trust in the way God asks us to live.

Stewardship means giving God's way, according to your means and God's standards. It means recognizing the blessings you have received, and acknowledging that you are the trustee of those blessings, not the owner. And as a trustee of God's gifts, you are challenged to use them as God proposes, which can bring a radical new freedom and peace to your life.

God's way is proportionate giving: deciding from the outset to share a portion of your income with the Church and the needy as you return to God a portion of the blessings you have received. The standard of giving God has proposed is the tithe, or 10 percent of our income. For most of us, tithing may currently just be a goal we are striving to reach. Most important, however, is the fact that God's standard is proportionate. Each of us can apply it to ourselves no matter what our income, but it will require dedication and sacrifice.

Our stewardship of treasure renewal will include a special homily on Saturday and Sunday, (*give dates*). During the following week, you will receive, by mail, a Card of Intent which will give you the opportunity to voluntarily indicate your intention. You are asked to return your card through a special collection on Saturday and Sunday, (*give dates*). We are hoping for a 100 percent return of these cards. Even if you cannot increase your giving or, indeed, cannot give anything, please return your card with an intent to pray for the success of this program and our parish.

Please read the special bulletin inserts during the next few weeks, think about what you read, and pray for one another. I know we can count on the participation of everyone in our parish this year. I thank you in advance for your support.

In Christ, the Great Steward,

(Name and Signature of Pastor)

Sample Letter From Pastor—B

(PARISH LETTERHEAD)

Date

Dear (*name of parishioner*):

What makes you feel good? Most people would agree that one thing is when someone does something special for them, or when they do something special for others. These occurrences demonstrate a basic human need to give and receive love. This fundamental human need is the heart of Christian stewardship: God blesses us and, in gratitude, we return a portion to God.

Included with this letter is your stewardship of treasure Intent Card. Now is the time to choose what portion of your income you will return to God. This decision is between you and God; the design of the three-part Intent Card ensures this confidentiality.

Perhaps you are able to accept God's standard of the 10 percent tithe. Perhaps the full tithe is only a goal at this time in your life, so your proportionate giving may be only 8 percent, or 5 percent, or 3 percent of your income. According to God's own words in sacred Scriptures, you will be blessed for your sacrifice.

Please complete and return your Intent Cards in the proper enclosed envelopes at Mass this weekend (*give dates*), mail them in, or bring them to the rectory. We are striving for a 100 percent return of the cards, so anyone whose cards are not returned will receive a follow-up letter or phone call from a parish volunteer.

Thank you for your commitment to the future of our parish and our beloved Church, and may God continue to bless your good stewardship.

In Christ, the Great Steward,

(Name and Signature of Pastor)

P.S. The three-part Intent Cards are designed so that what you decide to give is between you and God. Part "A" tells the parish office only that your cards have been returned, so we know who may need a follow-up call. Notice that there is no space on Part "A" for the amount of your intent and no place for your name on Part "B." Please separate Part "A" from Part "B," seal them in their proper envelopes, and place them in the special collection on (*give dates*). We will tally the "A" cards, and total the dollar amounts on the "B" cards for parish budgeting purposes. Part "C" is yours to keep as a visible reminder of your stewardship intent.

YEAR Stewardship of Treasure Renewal – 1 **MONTH**

SUNDAY	MONDAY	TUESDAY	WEDNESDAY	THURSDAY	FRIDAY	SATURDAY
						Bullet Insert #1 ——— Pulpit Announce-ment
Bulletin Insert # 1 ——— Pulpit Announce-ment		Mail First Letter ("A") ——— Enclose Stewardship Flyer				Bulletin Insert #2 ——— Pulpit Announce-ment
Bulletin Insert # 2 ——— Pulpit Announce-ment						Bulletin Insert #3 ——— Pulpit Announce-ment
Bulletin Insert # 3 ——— Pulpit Announce-ment		Mail Second Letter ("B") ———				Special Brochure Insert ——— Stewardship Homily
Special Brochure Insert ——— Stewardship Homily		Mail Third Letter ("C") ——— Enclose A-B-C Intent Cards With A-B Envelopes				Bulletin Insert #4 ——— Intent Card Collection

YEAR Stewardship of Treasure Renewal – 2 **MONTH**

SUNDAY	MONDAY	TUESDAY	WEDNESDAY	THURSDAY	FRIDAY	SATURDAY
Bulletin Insert #4 ——— Intent Card Collection		Mail Fourth Letter "D" ——— Enclose Follow-Up Intent Cards & Envelopes				Follow-Up Intent Card Collection
Follow-Up Intent Card Collection		Mail Acknow-ledgment Letter ("E")	Telephone Committee Begins Follow-Up Phone Calls			
			Telephone Committee Completes Follow-Up Phone Calls			

(PARISH NAME)
STEWARDSHIP OF TREASURE RENEWAL
INFORMATION UPDATE CARD
(for parish records)

With hope and faith, I/we hereby submit my/our Stewardship of Treasure Intent:

Signature:____________________________ Date: ____________
PLEASE PRINT:
Name: ____
Address:_______________________________________
City:____________________________ State:_____ ZIP: ______

Please detach this card and place in the container for "Information Update Cards" at the designated time.

------------------------------------ Cut ------------------------------------

(PARISH NAME)
B
STEWARDSHIP OF TREASURE RENEWAL
CONFIDENTIAL INTENT CARD
(for budgeting purposes)

Date:____________

In prayerful thanksgiving for the many blessings bestowed upon me/us, I/we intend to contribute to (*name*) Parish:

$ ____________Weekly $ ____________Quarterly
$ ____________Monthly $ ____________ Annually

I assume that my health and personal affairs will permit me to carry out this intention and it is understood that I am the sole judge of these conditions. At any time I find any of them unfavorable, I will simply make necessary changes.

The information on this card is between you and God. **Please detach and place it in the container for "Intent Cards" at the designated time. This card will be destroyed.**

------------------------------------ Cut ------------------------------------

(PARISH NAME)
C
STEWARDSHIP OF TREASURE RENEWAL
PARISH REMINDER CARD
(for your records)

Date:____________

I/we intend the following as my/our Stewardship of Treasure:

$ ____________Weekly $ ____________Quarterly
$ ____________Monthly $ ____________ Annually

Please detach and keep this card for your own records.

Appendix 4

Proportional-Giving Grids

On the following pages, you will find grids that display weekly and annual proportional-giving amounts, based on gross annual income. Parishioners who choose tithing or proportional giving as an aspect of their discipleship can use these grids to determine the amount of their financial resources they will return to God. (See Chapters 9 and 10 for related materials.)

Proportional Giving by Week

Gross Ann.Inc.	1% Weekly	2% Weekly	3% Weekly	4% Weekly	5% Weekly	6% Weekly	7% Weekly	8% Weekly	9% Weekly	10% Weekly
$5,000	$0.96	$1.92	$2.88	$3.85	$4.81	$5.77	$6.73	$7.69	$8.65	$9.62
$10,000	$1.92	$3.85	$5.77	$7.69	$9.62	$11.54	$13.46	$15.38	$17.31	$19.23
$15,000	$2.88	$5.77	$8.65	$11.54	$14.42	$17.31	$20.19	$23.08	$25.96	$28.85
$20,000	$3.85	$7.69	$11.54	$15.38	$19.23	$23.08	$26.92	$30.77	$34.62	$38.46
$25,000	$4.81	$9.62	$14.42	$19.23	$24.04	$28.85	$33.65	$38.46	$43.27	$48.08
$30,000	$5.77	$11.54	$17.31	$23.08	$28.85	$34.62	$40.38	$46.15	$51.92	$57.69
$35,000	$6.73	$13.46	$20.19	$26.92	$33.65	$40.38	$47.12	$53.85	$60.58	$67.31
$40,000	$7.69	$15.38	$23.08	$30.77	$38.46	$46.15	$53.85	$61.54	$69.23	$76.92
$45,000	$8.65	$17.31	$25.96	$34.62	$43.27	$51.92	$60.58	$69.23	$77.88	$86.54
$50,000	$9.62	$19.23	$28.85	$38.46	$48.08	$57.69	$67.31	$76.92	$86.54	$96.15
$55,000	$10.58	$21.15	$31.73	$42.31	$52.88	$63.46	$74.04	$84.62	$95.19	$105.77
$60,000	$11.54	$23.08	$34.62	$46.15	$57.69	$69.23	$80.77	$92.31	$103.85	$115.38
$65,000	$12.50	$25.00	$37.50	$50.00	$62.50	$75.00	$87.50	$100.00	$112.50	$125.00
$70,000	$13.46	$26.92	$40.38	$53.85	$67.31	$80.77	$94.23	$107.69	$121.15	$134.62
$75,000	$14.42	$28.85	$43.27	$57.69	$72.12	$86.54	$100.96	$115.38	$129.81	$144.23
$80,000	$15.38	$30.77	$46.15	$61.54	$76.92	$92.31	$107.69	$123.08	$138.46	$153.85
$85,000	$16.35	$32.69	$49.04	$65.38	$81.73	$98.08	$114.42	$130.77	$147.12	$163.46
$90,000	$17.31	$34.62	$51.92	$69.23	$86.54	$103.85	$121.15	$138.46	$155.77	$173.08
$95,000	$18.27	$36.54	$54.81	$73.08	$91.35	$109.62	$127.88	$146.15	$164.42	$182.69
$100,000	$19.23	$38.46	$57.69	$76.92	$96.15	$115.38	$134.62	$153.85	$173.08	$192.31

Proportional Giving by Year

Gross Ann.Inc.	1% Annual	2% Annual	3% Annual	4% Annual	5% Annual	6% Annual	7% Annual	8% Annual	9% Annual	10% Annual
$5,000	$50.00	$100.00	$150.00	$200.00	$250.00	$300.00	$350.00	$400.00	$450.00	$500.00
$10,000	$100.00	$200.00	$300.00	$400.00	$500.00	$600.00	$700.00	$800.00	$900.00	$1,000.00
$15,000	$150.00	$300.00	$450.00	$600.00	$750.00	$900.00	$1,050.00	$1,200.00	$1,350.00	$1,500.00
$20,000	$200.00	$400.00	$600.00	$800.00	$1,000.00	$1,200.00	$1,400.00	$1,600.00	$1,800.00	$2,000.00
$25,000	$250.00	$500.00	$750.00	$1,000.00	$1,250.00	$1,500.00	$1,750.00	$2,000.00	$2,250.00	$2,500.00
$30,000	$300.00	$600.00	$900.00	$1,200.00	$1,500.00	$1,800.00	$2,100.00	$2,400.00	$2,700.00	$3,000.00
$35,000	$350.00	$700.00	$1,050.00	$1,400.00	$1,750.00	$2,100.00	$2,450.00	$2,800.00	$3,150.00	$3,500.00
$40,000	$400.00	$800.00	$1,200.00	$1,600.00	$2,000.00	$2,400.00	$2,800.00	$3,200.00	$3,600.00	$4,000.00
$45,000	$450.00	$900.00	$1,350.00	$1,800.00	$2,250.00	$2,700.00	$3,150.00	$3,600.00	$4,050.00	$4,500.00
$50,000	$500.00	$1,000.00	$1,500.00	$2,000.00	$2,500.00	$3,000.00	$3,500.00	$4,000.00	$4,500.00	$5,000.00
$55,000	$550.00	$1,100.00	$1,650.00	$2,200.00	$2,750.00	$3,300.00	$3,850.00	$4,400.00	$4,950.00	$5,500.00
$60,000	$600.00	$1,200.00	$1,800.00	$2,400.00	$3,000.00	$3,600.00	$4,200.00	$4,800.00	$5,400.00	$6,000.00
$65,000	$650.00	$1,300.00	$1,950.00	$2,600.00	$3,250.00	$3,900.00	$4,550.00	$5,200.00	$5,850.00	$6,500.00
$70,000	$700.00	$1,400.00	$2,100.00	$2,800.00	$3,500.00	$4,200.00	$4,900.00	$5,600.00	$6,300.00	$7,000.00
$75,000	$750.00	$1,500.00	$2,250.00	$3,000.00	$3,750.00	$4,500.00	$5,250.00	$6,000.00	$6,750.00	$7,500.00
$80,000	$800.00	$1,600.00	$2,400.00	$3,200.00	$4,000.00	$4,800.00	$5,600.00	$6,400.00	$7,200.00	$8,000.00
$85,000	$850.00	$1,700.00	$2,550.00	$3,400.00	$4,250.00	$5,100.00	$5,950.00	$6,800.00	$7,650.00	$8,500.00
$90,000	$900.00	$1,800.00	$2,700.00	$3,600.00	$4,500.00	$5,400.00	$6,300.00	$7,200.00	$8,100.00	$9,000.00
$95,000	$950.00	$1,900.00	$2,850.00	$3,800.00	$4,750.00	$5,700.00	$6,650.00	$7,600.00	$8,550.00	$9,500.00
$100,000	$1,000.00	$2,000.00	$3,000.00	$4,000.00	$5,000.00	$6,000.00	$7,000.00	$8,000.00	$9,000.00	$10,000.00

APPENDIX 5

Sample Parish Survey

On the following pages, you will find an excellent example of a parish survey which was developed by St. John the Baptist Parish in Newburgh, Indiana. We thank the staff members and volunteers from St. John's for their inspired creativity in producing this survey. (See Chapter 19 for related materials.)

Listening to Our Parish Family Needs Assessment

In an effort to know if existing programs are helpful to our families and if there are any important needs that are being missed, would you please help us serve you better by completing this survey. Please return the survey to us no later than **March 15, 1995**, by placing it in the collection basket or mailing to St. John Parish, 625 Frame Road, Newburgh, IN 47630.

Thank You!

Name (optional) ____

Age: 12–17______ 18–24 _____ 25–39 ______ 40–59 _____ 60–75 ____ 75+_____

Areas of Concern

WORSHIP SERVICES

1. I would like to learn new hymns. ___ yes ___ no
2. I would like to have a children's choir. ___ yes ___ no
3. The homilies are ___ good ___ okay ___ not so good.
4. I would like to hear a homily on ___________
5. I would like the greeters/ushers to wear name-tags. ___ yes ___ no
6. I like having baby-sitting during 8:45 and 11:00 Masses. ___ yes ___ no
7. I would like to ___ help with baby-sitting ___ join the choir.
8. Comments/suggestions _________________ ___________________________________

OTHER WORSHIP SERVICES/SACRAMENTS

1. Communion is brought to shut-ins often enough. ___ yes ___ no
2. We should have more than 3 parish penance services. ___ yes ___ no
3. I would like to have communal services for anointing of the sick more often than twice a year. ___ yes ___ no
4. Confirmation should be mandatory in the eighth grade. ___ yes ___ no
5. Comments/suggestions _________________ ___________________________________

EDUCATION

1. I am satisfied with St. John School. ___ yes ___ no ___ N/A
2. Greater effort should be made to strengthen the enrollment and finances of the school. ___ yes ___ no ___ N/A
3. The school does a good job of passing on the Catholic faith to our children. ___ yes ___ no ___ N/A
4. Having a teacher available to answer concerns during evening hours would be helpful. ___ yes ___ no ___ N/A
5. I am satisfied with the school's extracurricular activities (speech, sports, etc.). ___ yes ___ no ___ N/A
6. I am satisfied with the academic curriculum offered at St. John School. ___ yes ___ no ___ N/A
7. Childcare before and after kindergarten would be helpful. ___ yes ___ no ___ N/A
8. Preschool for 4-year-olds should be considered. ___ yes ___ no ___ N/A
9. I am interested in education at St. John School. ___ yes ___ no ___ N/A
10. Comments/suggestions _________________ ___________________________________

RELIGIOUS EDUCATION

1. I am satisfied with the grade-school religious education classes. ___ yes ___ no ___ N/A
2. I am satisfied with the high-school religious education classes. ___ yes ___ no ___ N/A
3. I am satisfied with the preschool religious education classes. ___ yes ___ no ___ N/A
4. Training for catechists is adequate. ___ yes ___ no ___ N/A
5. I am satisfied with the time/schedule of religious education classes. ___ yes ___ no ___ N/A
6. Adequate resources are available for these classes. ___ yes ___ no ___ N/A
7. Comments/suggestions _________________ ___________________________________

FINANCES

1. More information should be given to parishioners about how they can remember St. John Parish in their wills and other estate planning. ___ yes ___ no
2. The parish provides sufficient information on its finances. ___ yes ___ no
3. Major fund-raisers are needed in addition to the summer social. ___ yes ___ no
4. I would like more information on spiritual giving (proportional giving of my resources). yes ___ no
5. I would contribute more if _______________
6. Comments/suggestions _________________ ___________________________________

ADULT EDUCATION

1. The RCIA program is satisfactory.
   ___ yes ___ no ___ N/A
2. I would like more information about RCIA.
   ___ yes ___ no ___ N/A
3. Efforts to reach out for converts to the Catholic faith are adequate. ___ yes ___ no
4. A program for "cradle Catholics" to learn more about their faith would be helpful. ___ yes ___ no
5. If available, I ___ would (___would not) participate in a support group for mothers of toddlers ___grade-school children ___teenagers.
6. If available, I ___ would (___would not) participate in a support group for parents of toddlers ___grade-school children ___teenagers.
7. I would like to see more family programs (like the Advent festival) take place at St. John.
   ___ yes ___ no
8. I know about the FOCUS program.
   ___ yes ___ no
9. Topics for the FOCUS program might be
   ____
10. FACE-TO-FACE is a helpful program for men.
    ___ yes ___ no
11. The topic of women's spirituality interests me.
    ___ yes ___ no
12. The parish offers adequate Bible study sessions.
    ___ yes ___ no
13. Weekend retreats/workshops are adequate.
    ___ yes ___ no
14. Issues that concern me are
    __ education in human sexuality
    __ marriage enrichment
    __ help for hurting marriages
    __ parenting support and skills
    __balancing work and home
15. I am interested in a vocation to the priesthood/ religious life. ___ yes ___ no
16. Comments/suggestions ________________
    ____
    ____

FACILITIES

1. I am proud of our facilities. ___ yes ___ no
2. The buildings are usually clean. ___ yes ___ no
3. The buildings are well-maintained.
   ___ yes ___ no
4. Something in need of cleaning is __________
5. Something in need of repair is ___________
6. I am satisfied with the usage of the buildings.
   ___ yes ___ no
7. St. John needs additional space for _________
8. Comments/suggestions ________________
   ____
   ____

COMMUNITY OUTREACH/ CHRISTIAN SERVICE

1. Local efforts to help the poor are adequate
   ___ yes ___ no
2. The parish should sponsor ecumenical activities with other neighborhood churches.
   ___ yes ___ no
3. The parish is active in peace and justice issues.
   ___ yes ___ no
4. Comments/suggestions ________________
   ____
   ____

WELCOME/FELLOWSHIP

1. St. John is a welcoming, warm community.
   ___ yes ___ no
2. Welcoming of newcomers to the parish is satisfactory. ___ yes ___ no
3. St. John should do more for visitors.
   ___ yes ___ no
4. Social activities at the parish are adequate.
   ___ yes ___ no
5. Comments/suggestions ________________
   ____
   ____

GENERAL COMMENTS

1. St. John Parish has adequate staffing.
   ___ yes ___ no
2. Staff members are competent. ___ yes ___ no
3. What I like least about St. John Parish is ____
   ____
4. A change/improvement/addition I would like to see implemented at St. John Parish is _______
   ____
5. I attend this parish because
   __ meets my spiritual needs
   __ children go to school here
   __ convenient Mass times
   __ assigned parish
   __ liturgy
   __ music
   __ proximity
   __ clergy
   __ warmth of parish
   __ other (specify) ______________
6. I have skills/talents and would like to volunteer my services in the following areas:
   __ greeter
   __ lector
   __ usher
   __ eucharistic minister
   __ adult education
   __ religious education
   __ clerical
   __ computer
   __ maintenance
   __ mailings
   __ church cleaner
   __ other (specify) ______________
7. What I like most about St. John Parish is
   ____
   ____
8. I would like prayers for ________________
   ____
   ____

APPENDIX 6

Sample Planned-Giving Society and Parish-Endowment Brochures

On the following pages, you will find outstanding examples of a parish planned-giving society brochure and a parish-endowment brochure, which were created and produced by St. Anthony of Padua Parish in Evansville, Indiana (see Chapters 12, 14, and 15). Thanks and congratulations to St. Anthony's staff members and volunteers for their initiative and ingenuity.

Sample Planned-Giving Society Brochure

Sample Planned-Giving Society Brochure

The Paduan Society is an organization of very special friends of historic St. Anthony Church.

OBJECTIVE OF THE SOCIETY

- To recognize friends and members who have made a financial provision for St. Anthony Church in their estate plans.
- To help perpetuate and extend the mission of St. Anthony Church throughout our community.
- To facilitate and enhance members' interest and participation in St. Anthony Church.

MEMBERSHIP

1. Membership in the Paduan Society is open to all friends of St. Anthony Church who provide for the future of the parish through a planned gift. Your gift may be a bequest in your will of cash, stocks, bonds, or other property. You could also make the Church the beneficiary of an IRA or a life-insurance policy. Other planned-giving techniques could be used as well.
2. You may also become a member by making a single gift of $1,000 or more during your lifetime to the St. Anthony Catholic Church Endowment.

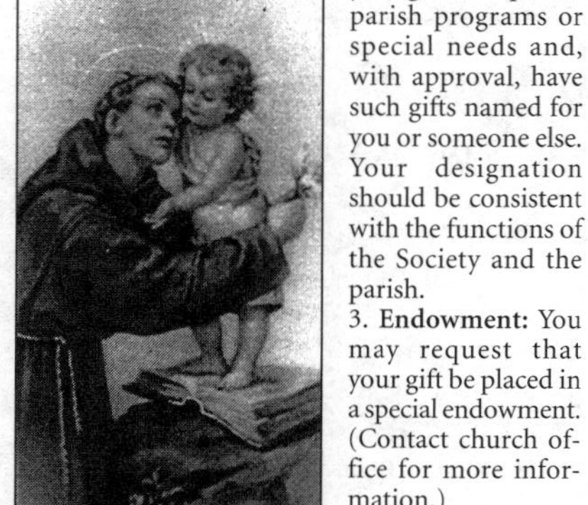

EVERY GIFT IS IMPORTANT TO THE FUTURE OF ST. ANTHONY CHURCH

Donors may choose any of the following options:

1. **Unrestricted gifts:** Your gifts may be used for general support, or for a special purpose or program exhibiting the greatest need as determined by the parish leadership.
2. **Restricted gifts:** You may designate your gifts for specific parish programs or special needs and, with approval, have such gifts named for you or someone else. Your designation should be consistent with the functions of the Society and the parish.
3. **Endowment:** You may request that your gift be placed in a special endowment. (Contact church office for more information.)

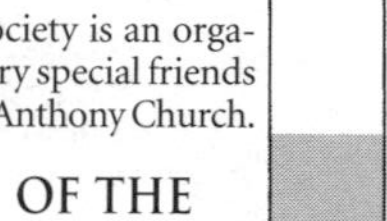

The Paduan Society is dedicated to the ideals and mission of the Roman Catholic Church and St. Anthony Parish, Evansville, Indiana.

The Society is named for St. Anthony of Padua, born in 1195. He became an Augustinian monk at age fifteen and, ten years later, joined the Franciscan Order, becoming the provincial of a group of monasteries for that order in 1227.

In 1230 he resigned his provincialship to devote more time to preaching. One year after his death in 1231, he was canonized by Pope Gregory IX. In 1946, he was named Doctor of the Church. Saint Anthony is the saint invoked for finding lost articles. His feast day is June 13.

Sample Parish-Endowment Brochure

REQUEST FOR ADDITIONAL INFORMATION

Name ______________

Address ______________

City ____ State ____ ZIP ____

Phone ______________

__ Enclosed is my check or other donation to the St. Anthony (Evansville) Endowment.

__ I have named the Endowment in my

- __ Will
- __ Pension plan
- __ IRA
- __ Trust Fund
- __ Insurance Policy
- __ Annuity
- __ Other

__ I would like more information. Please contact me.

Mail this portion and any donation to

St. Anthony Catholic Church
704 First Avenue
Evansville, IN 47710
Phone: 812/423-5209

ST. ANTHONY CATHOLIC CHURCH ENDOWMENT BENEFITS

- St. Anthony will receive income from the endowment forever.
- The mission of St. Anthony Parish will be perpetuated.
- The historical buildings of St. Anthony Parish will be preserved and enjoyed by future generations.
- You will receive attractive tax benefits.

...FOR THE REST OF TIME

ST. ANTHONY CATHOLIC CHURCH ENDOWMENT

Sample Parish-Endowment Brochure

SOME HISTORICAL HIGHLIGHTS...

When Mrs. Magdalena Reis in 1885 donated land in what is now the downtown corridor of Evansville, who would have thought she was establishing a cornerstone of giving for one of the oldest Catholic Churches in Indiana. Three years later, St. Anthony Parish was established.

On June 13, 1888, the feast of St. Anthony of Padua, the first parish Mass was celebrated in the attic of the Reis home. Mass was celebrated there until June 1889 when the first parish building was dedicated. This first parish building was both church and school until 1896 when the present St. Anthony Catholic Church was completed. Today, the Reis home is the parish rectory and office.

In 1888, St. Anthony was a parish of German immigrants. St. Anthony Parish is now situated in an American melting pot in a changing neighborhood. The area in which St. Anthony is located is in the midst of a major transformation from small, single-family dwellings on quiet, tree-lined streets, to a blend of private residences and commercial properties on busy thoroughfares.

St. Anthony Parish is a stable center for praise to a glorious God and a safe refuge for the less fortunate of our society. The future is bright and exciting for this historic jewel.

THE ST. ANTHONY CATHOLIC CHURCH ENDOWMENT

The St. Anthony Endowment has been established to perpetuate and extend the mission of St. Anthony Parish throughout the community. An endowment is money or other donated gifts which are invested to produce perpetual income for a particular purpose. The St. Anthony Endowment will be used to enhance, enrich, and continue the mission of St. Anthony Catholic Church: *"We are called to be a faith-filled family who acts justly, loves tenderly, forgives freely, and walks humbly with our God."*

A GIFT TO THE ENDOWMENT

Gifts can be made to the endowment in a number of ways:

- ***Cash:*** donate currency or write a check to the St. Anthony Catholic Church Endowment
- ***Bequests:*** donate a percent or a stated dollar amount in your will
- ***Real Estate:*** donate land, a home, or buildings
- ***Life Estate:*** donate real estate but live in your home or benefit from rental property during your lifetime
- ***Life Insurance:*** name the Endowment as a full or partial beneficiary on a new or existing policy
- ***Annuities:*** the Endowment can be designated to receive any residual benefits
- ***Personal Property:*** donate art work, jewelry, or other valuables
- ***Stock:*** transfer stock or other securities
- ***IRAs and Other Pension Plans:*** designate the Endowment as the beneficiary to receive the proceeds of your pension plan or IRA
- ***Other:*** investigate other methods of donation by calling the St. Anthony Church office

BENEFITS OF DONATING TO THE ENDOWMENT

For the rest of time...Not only will St. Anthony Parish benefit from your gift to the endowment, you will receive many benefits as well.

- You will know that you are helping support and sustain the mission of St. Anthony Catholic Church.
- Donating to the endowment ensures that your gift will give forever, providing St. Anthony with income for the *rest of time.*
- Your gift will qualify for attractive tax benefits.
- Your gift will be pooled with other endowment donations for advantageous investing and cost-efficient management.

Appendix 7

Ten Characteristics of a Total Stewardship Parish

1. ***Public Commitment by Parish Leaders:*** The pastor, parish staff, parish council, finance committee, and others commit to a continuous stewardship-conversion process that is reflected in the parish mission statement and/or long-range plan.

2. ***Active, Dynamic Stewardship Conversion Committee:*** This committee actively directs and monitors the parish's stewardship-conversion endeavors.

3. ***Year-Round Spiritual Formation and Educational Activities:*** These education and formation activities remind all parishioners of their responsibility to be Christ's disciples in their homes, workplaces, and communities, and expose them—womb to tomb—to the Church's teachings about stewardship.

4. ***Annual Time, Talent, and Treasure Renewals:*** These renewals compel parishioners to share their gifts primarily as a faith response, but also as a way to help meet the needs of the parish, the local community, and the world.

5. ***Total-Stewardship Financial Plan:*** This total-stewardship financial plan includes the following elements: (1) parishioners—including children—use envelopes supplied by the parish for their church offerings; (2) tithing or proportional giving is promoted as the norm for stewardship of

treasure; (3) incremental movement toward eliminating second collections, special envelopes, and supplementary fund-raisers for ordinary parish operating expenses; (4) parish campaigns for extraordinary capital improvements/repairs, new building projects, or debt reduction, diocesan appeal, and so on, are conducted according to the Church's teachings and practices of stewardship; (5) long-term financial security of the parish is being ensured through planned gifts and endowments placed with the diocesan foundation; (6) no school tuition (when applicable); (7) parish publishes an annual accountability report for its stewardship of treasure; also publishes monthly or quarterly updates of its budget.

6. ***Contributes a Portion of Its Weekly Offertory Collection to Other Parishes:*** The parish gives part of its collection to Christian social ministries and/or worthy community, regional, national or international programs; encourages parishioners' time and talent contributions outside the parish.

7. ***Comprehensive Communication System:*** A stewardship-conversion parish employs a comprehensive communication system whereby all parishioners are kept up-to-date regarding every aspect of parish life; includes a monthly newsletter that is mailed to every parish household.

8. ***Aggressive Hospitality Program:*** An aggressive hospitality program exists for creating parish ownership; welcoming members, newcomers and visitors; and acknowledging and thanking parishioners for gratefully returning to God a portion of their God-given time, talent, and treasure.

9. ***Total Prayer Life:*** A stewardship-conversion parish is characterized by a total prayer life that includes (1) intentional planning for, and evaluation of, all eucharistic and other liturgical and paraliturgical celebrations; (2) time set aside for prayer at all parish/school events, games, celebrations, and so on; and (3) multiple prayer and spiritual growth opportunities throughout the week, such as public recitation of the rosary, exposition of the Blessed Sacrament, prayer chains, Scripture study groups, family prayer in the home, and so on.

10. ***Value-Added Service Philosophy:*** A stewardship-conversion parish is seen as an extension of the nuclear family whose members work, play, and pray together, and help one another in good times and bad. This includes periodic, structured feedback opportunities regarding needs that are, and are not, being met, status of programs and services, quality of liturgies, and so on.

APPENDIX 8

Memorial and Honor Giving: Sample Materials

On the following pages, you will find samples of the types of materials needed to conduct a successful Memorial and Honor Giving Program. (See Chapter 12 for related materials.)

Sample: Memorial/Honor Gift Form

— MEMORIAL/HONOR GIFT FORM —

Amt: $ ____________________
Given by ____________________
Street/RFD/Box City State ZIP

For Memorial Gift: ____________________
Name of Deceased City

For Honor Gift: ____________________
Name of Honored Person(s) City

Occasion: ____________________
Fill in type of occasion or reason for gift (e.g. birthday, anniversary, friendship, etc.)

Send Acknowledgment Card(s) to ____________________

Mail your tax-deductible gift with the completed form to
— Parish Name and Address here —
Please send me additional forms ❑ pad of 5 ❑ pad of 10

Sample: Official Receipt
(mailed with follow-up letters)

Logo Here

OFFICIAL GIFT RECEIPT

Parish Name and Address

Receipt # ____________
Date ____________
Official Initials ____________

Donor(s) ____________
Address ____________
City/State/ZIP ____________
Amount/Value $ ____________

Type of Gift:
❑ Cash
❑ Other (specify) ____________

❑ Memorial Gift ❑ Honor Gift ❑ Other

THANK YOU FOR SUPPORTING THE WORK OF (*NAME*) PARISH
— PLEASE SAVE THIS RECEIPT FOR TAX PURPOSES —

Sample: Promotional Brochure (2 sides)

HONOR YOUR FRIENDS
OR LOVED ONES AND…
HELP
(*NAME*)
PARISH

Logo Here

It's often difficult to know how to express your respect and sympathy when a friend or loved one dies, or what to do for people close to you who are celebrating a special event or milestone in their lives.

One excellent way is through a MEMORIAL or HONOR GIFT to (*name*) Parish.

Bereaved families of those you have memorialized, or those you have honored because of special events in their lives, will immediately be notified of your gift with a beautiful card — and their names will be listed (without mentioning the amount given) in a future issue of the (*name*) Parish Newsletter.

MEMORIAL AND HONOR GIFTS TO (*NAME*) CAN HELP YOU

Your dollars do double duty with Memorial and Honor Giving. You properly care for a personal obligation and at the same time help (*name*) Parish continue its important programs and services.

They're private and noncompetitive: You don't have to "keep up with the Joneses." The amount of your gift is completely confidential, and the same acknowledgment card is sent to the bereaved family or honored persons regardless of the size of the gift.

They're simple and convenient: You won't need to spend hours looking for "just the right gift" and greeting card.

They're tax deductible: Within two weeks after you have been notified by mail that (*name*) Parish has received your gift, and that the bereaved family or honored persons have been notified of your gift, you will receive an official tax-deductible receipt.

USE THIS HANDY FORM NOW OR SAVE IT FOR LATER USE. →

Notice that there is a place on the bottom of the form for you to order an additional supply.

Remember that your friends might appreciate knowing about Memorial and Honor Gifts to (*name*) parish.

— MEMORIAL/HONOR GIFT FORM —

Amt: $ ____________________
Given by ____________________
Street/RFD/Box City State ZIP

For Memorial Gift: ____________________
Name of Deceased City

For Honor Gift: ____________________
Name of Honored Person(s) City

Occasion: ____________________
Fill in type of occasion or reason for gift (e.g. birthday, anniversary, friendship, etc.)

Send Acknowledgment Card(s) to ____________________

Mail your tax deductible gift with the completed form to
— Parish Name and Address here —
Please send me additional forms ❑ pad of 5 ❑ pad of 10

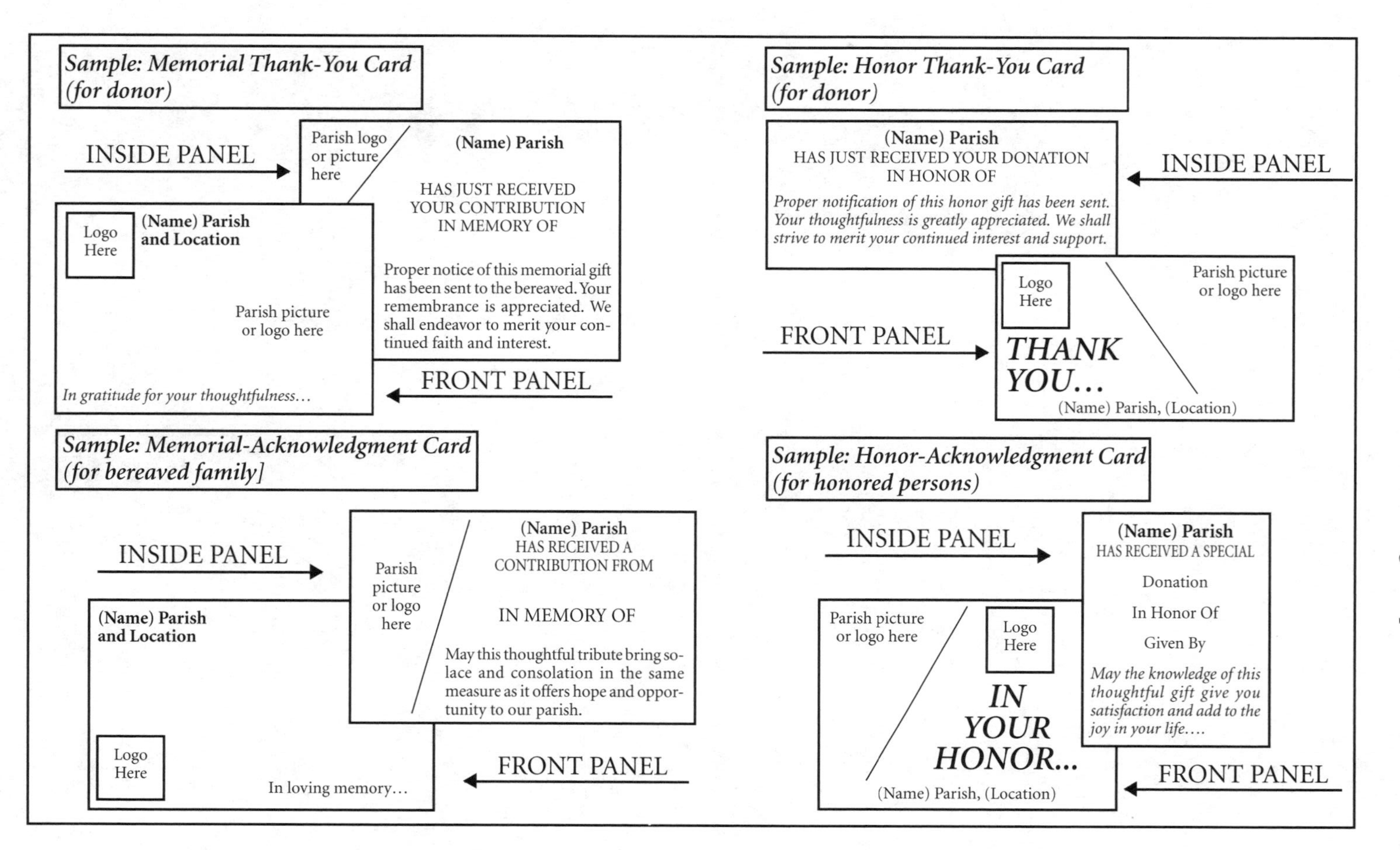

Sample: Memorial Thank-You Card (for donor)
INSIDE PANEL
Parish logo or picture here
(Name) Parish
HAS JUST RECEIVED YOUR CONTRIBUTION IN MEMORY OF
Proper notice of this memorial gift has been sent to the bereaved. Your remembrance is appreciated. We shall endeavor to merit your continued faith and interest.
Logo Here
(Name) Parish and Location
Parish picture or logo here
In gratitude for your thoughtfulness…
FRONT PANEL
Sample: Memorial-Acknowledgment Card (for bereaved family]
INSIDE PANEL
Parish picture or logo here
(Name) Parish
HAS RECEIVED A CONTRIBUTION FROM
IN MEMORY OF
May this thoughtful tribute bring solace and consolation in the same measure as it offers hope and opportunity to our parish.
(Name) Parish and Location
Logo Here
In loving memory…
FRONT PANEL
Sample: Honor Thank-You Card (for donor)
(Name) Parish
HAS JUST RECEIVED YOUR DONATION IN HONOR OF
Proper notification of this honor gift has been sent. Your thoughtfulness is greatly appreciated. We shall strive to merit your continued interest and support.
INSIDE PANEL
FRONT PANEL
Logo Here
Parish picture or logo here
THANK YOU…
(Name) Parish, (Location)
Sample: Honor-Acknowledgment Card (for honored persons)
INSIDE PANEL
(Name) Parish
HAS RECEIVED A SPECIAL
Donation
In Honor Of
Given By
May the knowledge of this thoughtful gift give you satisfaction and add to the joy in your life….
Parish picture or logo here
Logo Here
IN YOUR HONOR…
(Name) Parish, (Location)
FRONT PANEL

APPENDIX 9

The QBQ, or the Quickie Board Quiz

See Chapters 17 and 19 for related materials.

First Impressions: Part 1

THE ORGANIZATION

- Does your organization have…
  ___ Mission/Philosophy/Vision Statement?
  ___ Functional Strategic Plan?
  ___ Bylaws, Articles of Incorporation and Related Policies and Procedures?
  ___ Up-to-Date Personnel Policies With Job Descriptions?
  ___ Marketing/Fund Raising Plans With Related Materials?
  ___ Board Member Job Descriptions and/or Statement of Expectations for Board Members?
  ___ All Necessary Legalities (IRS, Nondiscrimination Policy, and so on)?

First Impressions: Part 2

THE BOARD OF DIRECTORS

- What about your board's…
  ___ size?
  ___ training program?
  ___ mix/balance?
  ___ committees?
  ___ plans: long- and short-range?

In-Depth Evaluation

- Are your board members…
  ___ committed?
  ___ in charge?
  ___ aware?
  ___ knowledgeable?
  ___ organized?
  ___ flexible?

APPENDIX 10

Director of Volunteerism: Sample Job Description

Education/Background

1. Some post-secondary education and experience; bachelors' or associate degree preferred.
2. Desirable areas of formal education and training: Communications, Public Relations, Personnel Management.

Job Responsibilities

1. Maintain and publicize master schedule for all parish events and projects.
   - Sample activities:
     - (a) Develop computerized scheduling system.
     - (b) Establish communication links with all parish staff members and volunteer leaders.
     - (c) Print schedules in newsletters and bulletins, display on parish bulletin boards, and so on.

2. Oversee the preparation of facilities for use by parish volunteer groups.
   - Sample activities:
     (a) Arrange for ample, clean, comfortable space for all meetings and programs.
     (b) Prepare refreshments as needed.
     (c) Provide all necessary equipment and materials.

3. Coordinate annual stewardship of time and talent renewals.
   - Sample activities:
     (a) Establish project calendar for each renewal period.
     (b) Oversee preparation of printed materials.
     (c) Coordinate and confirm follow-ups for everyone who "signs up" for a volunteer activity or project.

4. Participate in the development and supervision of a comprehensive communications plan for the parish.
   - Sample activities:
     (a) Oversee publication of a parish newsletter.
     (b) Develop phone trees for volunteer groups.
     (c) Conduct direct-mail campaigns as needed.

5. Plan and organize ministry fairs.
   - Sample activities:
     (a) Oversee preparation of the facility where fairs will be held.
     (b) Coordinate and assign exhibit spaces for each volunteer entity.
     (c) Direct parish-wide advertising/promotional campaign.

6. Prepare and maintain a parish directory.
   - Sample activities:
     (a) Oversee the collection of materials and information about all aspects of parish life.
     (b) Supervise the organization of the materials and information (above) in preparation for printing.
     (c) Prepare data for the pastor and parish council to assist in their decision to produce the directory "in-house" or to engage a professional church directory company.

7. Provide training and education, as needed, for volunteers and paid staff members.
   - Sample activities:
     (a) Develop and maintain a "parish volunteer center" with relevant, up-to-date printed material and audiovisual resources.
     (b) Schedule workshops and seminars designed to give parish volunteers and staff members the skills and information they need to successfully conduct their endeavors.
     (c) Supervise and train professional staff members and volunteer leaders in the most effective methods for working with, motivating, evaluating, and dismissing volunteers.

8. Assist in the development of succession plans for all volunteer groups and organizations.
   - Sample activities:
     (a) Help volunteer groups create manuals or handbooks that describe in detail the "who-what-where-how-and-whys" of their spheres of activities.
     (b) Use the DOV office as a repository for the bylaws and operational guidelines of parish organizations.
     (c) Maintain role descriptions for all volunteer leadership positions.

9. Provide support and direction for all efforts to recruit and match volunteers to each organization.
   - Sample activities:
     (a) Use parish computer system to collect and catalog information about parishioners' jobs, interests, hobbies, and so on.
     (b) Serve as parish archivist for organizational records and minutes of meetings.

10. Establish structures for determining parish needs.
    - Sample activities:
      (a) Conduct regular global surveys.
      (b) Direct-parish canvassing and census updates.
      (c) Create and maintain a "suggestion box" system.

11. Help organizations develop short- and long-range plans; store these plans in a central repository.
    - Sample activities:
        (a) Encourage and direct the creation of mission statements for parish organizations.
        (b) Facilitate long-range planning processes for parish groups as needed.

APPENDIX 11

A Wills Seminar Primer

A wills seminar is a two-hour program devoted to the broad issues and features relating to the preparation of a legal will. Sponsoring an annual wills seminar is an excellent way for a parish to promote estate planning and deferred giving as elements of the stewardship of treasure.

Benefits

Wills seminars offer multiple benefits for a parish and its members. Chief among the benefits is the simple fact that parishioners love them! A wills seminar is an outstanding example of the highest level of service which a parish can offer its people. It's a marvelous opportunity for people to grasp the importance of having a will, to learn about how a will is constructed, and to allay any misgivings about the process of creating a will.

Other benefits include:

- Provides a starting point for a parish's estate planning/deferred giving program, or a shot in the arm for an existing program.
- Strengthens the link between a parish and its members (significant public-relations value).
- Creates awareness about a potential significant source of funds for the parish.
- Provides opportunities for volunteers (attorneys, accountants, and so on) to share their time and talent.

- Opens the door for future seminars for parishioners who are interested in exploring some of the more exotic estate-planning strategies.

Preparation

The following issues and concerns should be addressed during the planning for a wills seminar:

Logistics

- Where will the seminar take place?
  - Comfortable room with tables and chairs
  - Provide all necessary audiovisual aids
  - Good public-address system (test beforehand)
  - Ask guests to sign in when they arrive
  - Nametags are optional (but nice)
  - Display a wide variety of appropriate handouts
  - Provide drinks and snacks during the break
  - Provide notepaper and pencils

Who Will Present the Information

- Principal presenter should be an attorney—preferably a volunteer who is a member of the parish—with a good grasp of current state and federal laws which pertain to drafting and updating wills.
- Main presenter could be assisted by other financial professionals, such as accountants, bank trust officers, financial planners, and so on.

When Is the Best Time to Schedule a Wills Seminar?

- Timing should be based on a working knowledge of parishioners' lifestyles.
- Monday through Thursday evenings are generally best for most people.
- Sunday mornings (after Mass) or Sunday afternoons often work well for many seniors who prefer not to travel after dark.
- Whatever timing is decided on, always provide childcare; parents with young children should be intensely interesting in having an up-to-date will because of guardianship issues in event of a tragic loss of the parents' lives.

Marketing

For several weeks prior to the seminar, employ every promotional medium available in the parish to advertise the seminar: newsletters, bulletins, posters, pulpit announcements, direct mail, and so on.

Seminar Agenda

- Open with a brief prayer service.
- Attorney answers the usual kinds of questions: About forty-five minutes
  - What is a will?
  - Who needs a will?
  - Why have a will?
  - What if I already have a will?
  - What if I die without a will?
  - How much does will preparation cost?
  - Can I make my own will?
  - What about probate?
  - What are "living wills"?
- Break (with hospitality): About fifteen minutes
- Questions and answers: About forty-five minutes
- Briefly introduce the topics of estate planning and deferred giving and mention that, if there is enough interest, the parish will sponsor future programs on these topics.
- Close the formal program with appropriate acknowledgments.
- Attorneys and other professionals in attendance should be asked to remain for an additional half-hour following the formal program to answer informal questions.

APPENDIX 12

Stewardship: A Disciple's Response

Introduction

Three convictions in particular underlie what we say in this pastoral letter.

1. Mature disciples make a conscious, firm decision, carried out in action, to be followers of Jesus Christ no matter the cost to themselves.
2. Beginning in conversion, change of mind and heart, this commitment is expressed not in a single action, nor even in a number of actions over a period of time, but in an entire way of life. It means committing one's very self to the Lord.
3. Stewardship is an expression of discipleship, with the power to change how we understand and live out our lives. Disciples who practice stewardship recognize God as the origin of life, the giver of freedom, the source of all they have and are and will be. They are deeply aware of the truth that, "The Lord's are the earth and its fullness; the world and those who dwell in it" (Ps 24:1). They know themselves to be recipients and caretakers of God's many gifts. They are grateful for what they have received and eager to cultivate their gifts out of love for God and one another.

The Challenge

In some ways it may be harder to be a Christian steward today than at times in the past.

Although religious faith is a strong force in the lives of many Americans, our country's dominant secular culture often contradicts the values of the Judeo-Christian tradition. This is a culture in which destructive "isms"—materialism, relativism, hedonism, individualism, consumerism—exercise seductive, powerful influences. There is a strong tendency to privatize faith, to push it to the margins of society, confining it to people's hearts or, at best, their homes, while excluding it from the marketplace of ideas where social policy is formed and men and women acquire their view of life and its meaning.

The Choice

Christians are part of this culture, influenced by it in many ways.

In recent decades many Catholics in particular have entered into the mainstream of American society. That has been a remarkable achievement. Often, though, this process also has widened the "split" between faith and life which Vatican II saw as one of "the more serious errors of our age" (*Gaudium et Spes,* 43). Thus American Catholicism itself has taken on some of the less attractive values of the secular culture.

For example, although religious people often speak about community, individualism infects the religious experience of many persons. Parishes, dioceses and church institutions appear impersonal and alienating in the eyes of many. Evangelization is not the priority it should be. How to use people's gifts and charisms, how to empower the laity, how to recognize the role of women, how to affirm racial, cultural and ethnic minorities, how to overcome poverty and oppression—these and countless other issues remain vexing questions, as well as opportunities.

Also, while many Catholics are generous in giving of themselves and their resources to the church, others do not respond to the needs in proportion to what they possess. The result now is a lack of resources which seriously hampers the church's ability to carry out its mission and obstructs people's growth as disciples.

This pastoral letter recognizes the importance of church support, including the sharing of time, talent and treasure. But it situates church support in its broader context—what it means to be a disciple of Jesus Christ.

This also is the context of stewardship. Generous sharing of resources, including money, is central to its practice, and church support is a necessary part of this. Essentially, it means helping the church's mission with money, time, personal resources of all kinds. This sharing is not an option for Catholics who understand what membership in the church involves. It is a serious duty. It is a consequence of the faith which Catholics profess and celebrate. This pastoral letter initiates a long-term, continuing process encouraging people to examine and interiorize stewardship's implications. At the start of this process it is important to lay out a comprehensive view of stewardship—a vision of a sharing, generous, accountable way of life rooted in Christian discipleship—which people can take to heart and apply to the circumstances of their lives. Concentrating on one specific obligation of stewardship, even one as important as church support, could make it harder—even impossible—for people to grasp the vision. It could imply that when the bishops get serious about stewardship, what they really mean is simply giving money.

The Vision

Jesus' invitation to follow him is addressed to people of every time and condition. Here and now it is addressed to us—Catholic citizens of a wealthy, powerful nation facing many questions about its identity and role in the waning years of a troubled century, members of a community of faith blessed with many human and material resources yet often uncertain about how to sustain and use them.

As bishops, we wish to present a vision which suits the needs and problems of the church in our country today and speaks to those who practice Christian stewardship in their particular circumstances.

What we say here is directed to ourselves as much as to you who read these words. As bishops, we recognize our obligation to be models of stewardship in all aspects of our lives. We must be stewards in our prayer and worship, in how we fulfill our pastoral duties in our custody of the church's doctrine, spiritual resources, personnel and funds, in our lifestyle and use of time, and even in such matters as the attention we give to personal health and recreation.

As we ask you to respond to the challenge of stewardship, we pray that we also will be open to the grace to respond. We pray that the Holy Spirit, whose gracious action conforms us to Jesus Christ and to the church, will enlighten us all and help us to renew our commitment as the Lord's disciples and as stewards of his bountiful gifts.

Plan of the Pastoral Letter

The pastoral letter proceeds according to the following plan.

I. *The Call.* Stewardship is part of discipleship. But Christian discipleship begins with vocation, the call to follow Jesus and imitate his way of life. The letter therefore begins with vocation. Then it presents a very general overview of stewardship considered in the context of discipleship, noting that people first of all are stewards of the personal vocations they receive from God. Discipleship and the practice of stewardship constitute a way of life which is both privileged and challenging.

II. *Jesus' Way.* Next the pastoral letter focuses more closely on the idea of stewardship, relying on the teaching and life of Jesus to probe its meaning. It considers the implications for disciples of Jesus engaged in stewardship. One of these is that all are called to evangelize, to share the good news with others. And what is the reward to which good stewards can look forward? The answer is perfect fulfillment in God's kingdom—a kingdom already present, real but imperfect, in this world, which Jesus' disciples help bring to its full reality by the practice of stewardship.

III. *Living as a Steward.* Having reflected in general terms upon Christian life considered from the point of view of discipleship and stewardship, the letter turns to the content of this way of life. It considers the content of life in relation to two human activities which are fundamental to the Christian vocation. The first is collaborating with God in the work of creation. The second is cooperating with God in the work of redemption. Both lie at the very heart of Christian stewardship in its deepest meaning.

IV. *Stewards of the Church.* The pastoral letter next considers the community of faith, the people of God, which is formed by the new covenant in and through Christ. Each member of the church shares in responsibility for its mission; each is called to practice stewardship of the church. Christians also are called to look outward and to place themselves at the service of the entire human community, especially those who are most in need. The eucharist is both the sign and the agent of this expansive communion of charity.

V. *The Christian Steward.* The letter closes with a brief portrait or profile of the Christian steward, drawn from the New Testament. In a special way the Blessed Virgin is the model of Christian discipleship and of the practice of Christian stewardship as it is understood here. Do we also wish to be disciples of Jesus Christ and to live in this way?

Who is a Christian disciple? One who responds to Christ's call, follows Jesus and shapes his or her life in imitation of Christ's. Who is a Christian steward? One who receives God's gifts gratefully, cherishes and tends them in a responsible and accountable manner, shares them in justice and love with others, and returns them with increase to the Lord.

Genesis tells us that God placed the first human beings in a garden to practice stewardship there—"to cultivate and care for it" (Gen 2:15). The world remains a kind of garden (or workshop, as some would prefer to say) entrusted to the care of men and women for God's glory and the service of humankind. In its simplest yet deepest sense, this is the Christian stewardship of which the pastoral letter speaks.

I. The Call

> As our concept of stewardship continues to evolve after 12 years of marriage, we are grateful for the people who have challenged us from the beginning to embrace fully Christ's teachings. They weren't always telling us the things we wanted to hear, but we feel blessed that we were able to work through the initial frustrations of committing the best portion of our time, talent and treasure to the church. It's difficult to separate ourselves from the demands and possessions of the world, but there's a tremendous amount of peace that comes from every decision we make for Christ and his will for us. We can't overstate the powerful impact the lifestyle has had on our marriage and three children.
>
> – Tom and LaNell Lilly,
> Owensboro, Kentucky

The Disciple's Vocation

The Christian vocation is essentially a call to be a disciple of Jesus. Stewardship is part of that. Even more to the point, however, Christians are called to be good stewards of the personal vocations they receive. Each of us must discern, accept and live out joyfully and generously the commitments, responsibilities and roles to which God calls him or her. The account of the calling of the first disciples, near the beginning of John's Gospel, sheds light on these matters.

John the Baptist is standing with two of his disciples—Andrew and, according to tradition, the future evangelist John—when Jesus passes by.

"Behold," John the Baptist exclaims, "the Lamb of God!" Wondering at these words, his companions follow Christ.

"What are you looking for?" Jesus asks them. "Rabbi," they say, "Where are you staying?" "Come and you will see." They spend the day with him, enthralled by his words and by the power of his personality.

Deeply moved by this experience, Andrew seeks out his brother Simon and brings him to Jesus. The Lord greets him: "You will be called Kephas"—Rock. The next day, encountering Philip, Jesus tells him: "Follow me." Philip finds his friend Nathanael and, challenging his skepticism, introduces him to the Lord. Soon Nathanael too is convinced: "Rabbi, you are the Son of God; you are the king of Israel."

This fast-paced narrative at the beginning of John's Gospel (Jn 1:35–50) teaches a number of lessons. For our purposes, two stand out.

One is the personal nature of a call from Jesus Christ. He does not summon disciples as a faceless crowd but as unique individuals. "How do you know me?" Nathanael asks. "Before Philip called you," Jesus answers, "I saw you under the fig tree." He knows people's personal histories, their strengths and weaknesses, their destinies; he has a purpose in mind for each one.

This purpose is individual vocation. "Only in the unfolding of the history of our lives and its events," says Pope John Paul II, "is the eternal plan of God revealed to each of us" *(Christifideles Laici,* 58). Every human life, every personal vocation, is unique.

And yet the vocations of all Christians do have elements in common. One of these is the call to be a disciple. In fact, we might say that to be disciples—to follow Christ and try to live his life as our own—*is* the common vocation of Christians; discipleship in this sense is Christian life.

The other lesson which John's narrative makes clear is that people do not hear the Lord's call in isolation from one another. Other disciples help mediate their vocations to them, and they in turn are meant to mediate the Lord's call to others. Vocations are communicated, discerned, accepted and lived out within a community of faith which is a community of disciples (cf. Pope John Paul II, *Redemptor Hominis,* 21); its members try to help one another hear the Lord's voice and respond.

Responding to the Call

Jesus not only calls people to him but also forms them and sends them out in his service (cf. Mt 10:5ff; Mk 6:7ff; Lk 9:1ff). Being sent on a mission is a consequence of being a disciple. Whoever wants to follow Christ will have much work to do on his behalf—announcing the good news and serving others as Jesus did.

Jesus' call is urgent. He does not tell people to follow him at some time in the future but here and now—at this moment, in these circumstances. There can be no delay. "Go and proclaim the kingdom of God....No one who sets a hand to the plow and looks to what was left behind is fit for the kingdom of God" (Lk 9:60, 62).

But a person can say no to Christ. Consider the wealthy and good young man who approaches Jesus asking how to lead an even better life. Sell your goods, Jesus tells him; give to the poor, and follow me. "When the young man heard this statement, he went away sad, for he had many possessions" (Mt 19:22).

Attachment to possessions is always more or less a problem, both for individuals and for the community of faith. In *The Long Loneliness* (New York: Doubleday, Image Books, 1959), written years after she became a Catholic, Dorothy Day recalls the "scandal" of encountering a worldly church—or, more properly, the worldliness of some Catholics: "business-like priests...collective wealth...lack of sense of responsibility for the poor." She concludes: "There was plenty of charity but too little justice" (p. 140).

The Call to Stewardship

Becoming a disciple of Jesus Christ leads naturally to the practice of stewardship. These linked realities, discipleship and stewardship, then make up the fabric of a Christian life in which each day is lived in an intimate, personal relationship with the Lord.

This Christ-centered way of living has its beginning in baptism, the sacrament of faith. As Vatican II remarks, all Christians are "bound to show forth, by the example of their lives and by the witness of their speech," that new life of faith which begins in baptism and is strengthened by the power of the Holy Spirit in confirmation *(Ad Gentes,* 11). Faith joins individuals and the community of Jesus' followers in intimacy with their Lord and leads them to live as his disciples. Union with Christ gives rise to a sense of solidarity and common cause between the disciples and the Lord, and also among the disciples themselves.

Refracted through the prisms of countless individual vocations, this way of life embodies and expresses the one mission of Christ: to do God's will, to proclaim the good news of salvation, to heal the afflicted, to care for one's sisters and brothers, to give life—life to the full—as Jesus did.

Following Jesus is the work of a lifetime. At every step forward, one is challenged to go further in accepting and loving God's will. Being a disciple is not just something else to do, alongside many other things suitable for Christians, it is a total way of life and requires continuing conversion.

Stewardship plays an important role in the lives of people who seek to follow Christ. In particular, as we have said, Christians must be stewards of their personal vocations, for it is these which show how, according to the circumstances of their individual lives, God wants them to cherish and serve a broad range of interests and concerns: life and health, along with their own intellectual and spiritual well-being and that of others; material goods and resources; the natural environment; the cultural heritage of humankind—indeed, the whole rich panoply of human goods, both those already realized and those whose realization depends upon the present generation or upon generations yet to come. Catholics have a duty, too, to be stewards of their church: that community of disciples, that body of Christ, of which they, individually and together, are the members, and in which "if one part suffers, all the parts suffer with it; if one part is honored, all the parts share its joy" (1 Cor 12:26).

The Cost of Discipleship

The way of discipleship is privileged beyond any other. Jesus says: "I came so that they might have life and have it more abundantly" (Jn 10:10). But discipleship is not an easy way. "If you wish to come after me," Jesus also says, "you must deny yourself and take up your cross daily and follow me. For if you wish to save your life you will lose it, but if you lose your life for my sake you will save it" (Lk 9:23–24).

The Lord's way is not a way of comfortable living or of what Dietrich Bonhoeffer, in *The Cost of Discipleship,* scornfully calls "cheap grace." This is not real grace but an illusion. It is what happens when people approach the following of Christ as a way to pleasant experiences and feeling good. Bonhoeffer contrasts this with "costly" grace. It is costly because it calls us to follow, and grace because it calls us to follow Jesus Christ. It is costly because it requires a disciple for Jesus' sake to put aside the craving for domination, possession and control, and grace because it confers true liberation and eternal life. It is costly, finally, because it condemns sin, and grace because it justifies the sinner.

But all this is very general. To understand and practice this way of life, people need models to imitate. These exist in abundance in the holy women and men who have gone before us in the faith; while our supreme source of guidance is found in the person and teaching of Jesus. Let us reflect on what he tells us about stewardship.

II. Jesus' Way

> Our parents are an inspiration to us as we look back on their lives of giving themselves for each other and for others. Had it not been for their lives of stewardship and giving, we would not perhaps have the faith we have today; and we want to pass that faith and love on to our children, grandchildren and others. And then our thoughts are turned to the ultimate sacrifice that Christ made for us. He did so, not because he had to, but because of his great love for us. And to think, all he asks in return is for us to love him and others! But it would mean little to tell someone we love them if we did not try to show that love in a concrete way.
>
> – Paul and Bettie Eck,
> Wichita, Kansas

The Example of Jesus

Jesus is the supreme teacher of Christian stewardship, as he is of every other aspect of Christian life; and in Jesus' teaching and life self-emptying is fundamental. Now, it might seem that self-emptying has little to do with stewardship, but in Jesus' case that is not so. His self-emptying is not sterile self-denial for its own sake; rather, in setting aside self, he is filled with the Father's will, and he is fulfilled in just this way: "My food is to do the will of the one who sent me and to finish his work" (Jn 4:34).

Jesus' mission is to restore to good order the created household of God which sin has disrupted. He not only perfectly accomplishes this task, but also, in calling disciples, empowers them to collaborate with him in the work of redemption for themselves and on behalf of others.

In describing the resulting way of life, Jesus does not waste time proposing lofty but unrealistic ideals; he tells his followers how they are expected to live. The Beatitudes and the rest of the Sermon on the Mount prescribe the lifestyle of a Christian disciple (cf. Mt 5:3—7:27). Although it does not suit worldly tastes, "the wisdom of this world is foolishness in the eyes of God" (1 Cor 3:19). One does well to live in this way. "Everyone who listens to these words of mine and acts on them will be like a wise man who built his house on a rock....Everyone who listens to these words of mine but does not act on them will be like a fool who built his house on sand" (Mt 7:24, 26).

The Image of the Steward

Jesus sometimes describes a disciple's life in terms of stewardship (cf. Mt 25:14–30, Lk 12:42–48), not because being a steward is the whole of it but because this role sheds a certain light on it. An *oikonomos* or steward is one to whom the owner of a household turns over responsibility for caring for the property, managing affairs, making resources yield as much as possible and sharing the resources with others. The position involves trust and accountability.

A parable near the end of Matthew's Gospel (cf. Mt 25:14–30) gives insight into Jesus' thinking about stewards and stewardship. It is the story of "a man who was going on a journey" and who left his wealth in silver pieces to be tended by three servants.

Two of them respond wisely by investing the money and making a handsome profit. Upon returning, the master commends them warmly and rewards them richly. But the third behaves foolishly, with anxious pettiness, squirreling away the master's wealth and earning nothing; he is rebuked and punished.

The silver pieces of this story stand for a great deal besides money. All temporal and spiritual goods are created by and come from God. That is true of everything human beings have: spiritual gifts like faith, hope and love, talents of body and brain, cherished relationships with family and friends, material goods, the achievements of human genius and skill, the world itself. One day God will require an accounting of the use each person has made of the particular portion of these goods entrusted to him or her.

Each will be measured by the standard of his or her individual vocation. Each has received a different "sum"—a unique mix of talents, opportunities, challenges, weaknesses and strengths, potential modes of service and response—on which the Master expects a return. He will judge individuals according to what they have done with what they were given.

St. Ignatius of Loyola begins his *Spiritual Exercises* with a classic statement of the "first principle and foundation" permeating this way of life. "Human beings," he writes, "were created to praise, reverence and serve God our Lord, and by this means to save their souls. The other things on the face of the earth are created for them to help them in attaining the end for which they are created. Hence they are to make use of these things in as far as they help them in the attainment of their end, and they must rid themselves of them in as far as they provide a hindrance to them....Our one desire and choice should be what is more conducive to the end for which we are created." St. Ignatius, fervently committed to the apostolate as he was, understood that the right use of things includes and requires that they be used to serve others.

What does all this say to busy people immersed in practical affairs? Is it advice only for those whose vocations lead them to withdraw from the world? Not as Jesus sees it: "But seek first the kingdom of God and his righteousness, and all these things will be given you besides" (Mt 6:33).

The Steward's Reward

People trying to live as stewards reasonably wonder what reward they will receive. This is not selfishness but an expression of Christian hope. Peter raises the question when he says to Jesus, "We have given up everything and followed you" (Mk 10:28).

Christ's response is more than Peter or any other disciple could reasonably hope or bargain for: "There is no one who has given up house or brothers or sisters or mother or father or children or lands for my sake and for the sake of the Gospel who will not receive a hundred times more now in this present age: houses and brothers and sisters and mothers and children and lands, with persecutions, and eternal life in the age to come" (Mk 10:29–30).

That is to say: Giving up means receiving more, including more responsibility as a steward; among the consequences of living this way will be persecution; and even though discipleship and stewardship set the necessary terms of Christian life in this world, they have their ultimate reward in another life.

Start, though, with the here and now. To be a Christian disciple is a rewarding way of life, a way of companionship with Jesus, and the practice of stewardship as a part of it is itself a source of deep joy. Those who live this way are happy people who have found the meaning and purpose of living.

For a long time religious believers—to say nothing of those who do not believe—have struggled with the question of what value to assign human activity. One solution is to consider it a means to an end: Do good here and now for the sake of a reward in heaven. Another solution passes over the question of an afterlife: Do good here and now for the sake of making this a better world.

Vatican Council II points to a third solution. It recognizes that human activity is valuable both for what it accomplishes here and now and also for its relationship to the hereafter. But, more important, it stresses not only the discontinuity between here and now and hereafter, but also the astonishing fact of continuity.

God's kingdom already is present in history, imperfect but real (cf. Mt. 10:7; *Lumen Gentium,* 48; *Gaudium et Spes,* 39). To be sure, it will come to fulfillment by God's power, on his terms, in his own good time. And yet, by their worthy deeds in this life, people also make a limited but real human contribution to building up the kingdom. They do so with an eye to present happiness and also to the perfect fulfillment which the kingdom—and themselves as part of it—will enjoy in the life to come. The council, therefore, teaches that the purpose of the human vocation to "earthly service" of one's fellow human beings is precisely to "make ready the material of the celestial realm" *(Gaudium et Spes,* 38).

In Christ, God has entered fully into human life and history. For one who is Christ's disciple there is no dichotomy, and surely no contradiction, between building the kingdom and serving human purposes as a steward does. These are aspects of one and the same reality—the reality called the Christian life.

God's kingdom is not an earthly kingdom, subject to decline and decay; it is the everlasting kingdom of the life to come. But that "life to come" is in continuity with this present life through the human goods, the worthy human purposes, which people foster now. And after people have done their best, God will perfect human goods and bring about the final fulfillment of human persons. "The throne of God and of the Lamb will be in it, and his servants will worship him. They will look upon his face, and his name will be on their foreheads. Night will be no more, nor will they need light from lamp or sun, for the Lord God shall give them light, and they shall reign forever and ever" (Rv 22:3–5).

III. Living as a Steward

I have learned to share because I want to, not because I need to. There are no controls, no strings attached and no guarantee when we give unconditionally. That doesn't mean that in retrospect I haven't questioned my decisions; it simply means that I've tried to look at it as a growth experience, always keeping in mind the life of Jesus Christ. I personally see stewardship as a nurturing process. It is in a sense an invitation to reassess our priorities. It is ongoing and often painful, but most of all it brings a personal sense of happiness and peace of mind as I continue my journey through life.

– Jim Hogan,
Green Bay, Wisconsin

Creation and Stewardship

Although it would be a mistake to think that stewardship by itself includes the whole of Christian life, in probing the Christian meaning of stewardship one confronts an astonishing fact: God wishes human beings to be his collaborators in the work of creation, redemption and sanctification; and such collaboration involves stewardship in its most profound sense. We exercise such stewardship, furthermore, not merely by our own power but by the power of the Spirit of truth, whom Jesus promises to his followers (cf. Jn 14:16–17) and whom we see at work at the first Pentecost inspiring the apostles to commence that proclamation of the good news which has continued to this day (cf. Acts 2:1–4).

The great story told in Scripture, the story of God's love for humankind, begins with God at work as Creator, maker of all that is: "In the beginning, when God created the heavens and the earth…" (Gen 1:1). Among God's creatures are human persons: "The Lord God formed man out of the clay of the ground and blew into his nostrils the breath of life" (Gen 2:7). God not only creates human beings, however, but bestows on them the divine image and likeness (cf. Gen 1:26). As part of this resemblance to God, people are called to cooperate with the Creator in continuing the divine work (cf. Pope John Paul II, *Laborem Exercens,* 25).

Stewardship of creation is one expression of this. The divine mandate to our first parents makes that clear. "Be fertile and multiply; fill the earth and subdue it. Have dominion over the fish of the sea, the birds of the air and all the living things that move on the earth" (Gen 1:28). Subduing and exercising dominion do not mean abusing the earth. Rather, as the second creation story explains, God settled humankind upon earth to be its steward—"to cultivate and care for it" (Gen 2:15).

This human activity of cultivating and caring has a generic name—work. It is not a punishment for or a consequence of sin. True, sin does painfully skew the experience of work: "By the sweat of your face shall you get bread to eat" (Gen 3:19). But, even so, God's mandate to humankind to collaborate with him in the task of creating—the command to work—comes *before* the fall. Work is a fundamental aspect of the human vocation. It is necessary for human happiness and fulfillment. It is intrinsic to responsible stewardship of the world.

So, as Vatican II observes, far from imagining that the products of human effort are "in opposition to God's power and that the rational creature exists as a kind of rival to the Creator," Christians see human achievements as "a sign of God's greatness and the flowering of his own mysterious design" *(Gaudium et Spes,* 34). While it is lived out by individual women and men in countless ways corresponding to their personal vocations, human cooperation with God's work of creation in general takes several forms.

Collaborators in Creation

One of these is a profound reverence for the great gift of life, their own lives and the lives of others, along with readiness to spend themselves in serving all that preserves and enhances life.

This reverence and readiness begin with opening one's eyes to how precious a gift life really is—and that is not easy, in view of our tendency to take the gift for granted. "Do any human beings ever realize life while they live it—every, every minute?" demands Emily in *Our Town.* And the stage manager replies, "No. The saints and poets, maybe—they do some" (Thornton Wilder, *Our Town* [New York: Harper & Row, 1958], p. 100). Yet it is necessary to make the effort. For Vatican II speaks of the "surpassing ministry of safeguarding life" and declares that "from the moment of its conception life must be guarded with the greatest care" *(Gaudium et Spes,* 51).

Partly, too, stewardship of the world is expressed by jubilant appreciation of nature, whose God-given beauty not even exploitation and abuse have destroyed.

And for all this, nature is never spent;
There lives the dearest freshness deep down things
And though the last lights off the black West went
Oh, morning, at the brown brink eastward springs—
Because the Holy Ghost over the bent
World broods with warm breast and with ah! bright wings.

– Gerard Manley Hopkins, "God's Grandeur,"
Poems of Gerard Manley Hopkins
(New York, Oxford University Press, 1950, p.70)

Beyond simply appreciating natural beauty, there is the active stewardship of ecological concern. Ecological stewardship means cultivating a heightened sense of human interdependence and solidarity. It therefore calls for renewed efforts to address what Pope John Paul calls "the structural forms of poverty" existing in this country and on the international level (Message for the World Day of Peace, January 1, 1990) And it underlines the need to reduce military spending and do away with war and weapons of war.

Especially this form of stewardship requires that many people adopt simpler lifestyles. This is true not only of affluent persons and societies, but also of those who may not be affluent as that term is commonly understood yet do enjoy access to superfluous material goods and comforts. Within the church, for example, it is important to avoid even the appearance of consumerism and luxury, and this obligation begins with us bishops. As Pope John Paul says, "Simplicity, moderation and discipline, as well as a spirit of sacrifice, must become a part of everyday life, lest all suffer the negative consequences of the careless habits of a few" (ibid.).

At the same time, life as a Christian steward also requires continued involvement in the human vocation to cultivate material creation. This productivity embraces art, scholarship, science and technology, as well as business and trade, physical labor, skilled work of all kinds and serving others. So-called ordinary work offers at least as many opportunities as do supposedly more glamorous occupations. A woman who works at a supermarket checkout counter writes: "I feel that my job consists of a lot more than ringing up orders, taking people's money and bagging their groceries....By doing my job well, I know I have a chance to do God's work too. Because of this, I try to make each of my customers feel special. While I'm serving them, they become the most important people in my life" (Maxine F. Dennis, in *Of Human Hands* [Minneapolis and Chicago: Augsburg Fortress and ACTA Publications, 1991], p.49).

Redemption and Stewardship

Everyone has some natural responsibility for a portion of the world and an obligation in caring for it to acknowledge God's dominion. But there are also those who might be called stewards by grace. Baptism makes Christians stewards of this kind, able to act explicitly on God's behalf in cultivating and serving the portion of the world entrusted to their care. We find the perfect model of such stewardship in the Lord. "For in him all the fullness was pleased to dwell, and through him to reconcile all things for him, making peace by the blood of his cross (Col 1:19–20); and finally it will be he who "hands over the kingdom to his God and Father" (1 Cor 15:24).

Although Jesus is the unique priest and mediator, his disciples share in his priestly work. Baptism makes them "a royal priesthood" (1 Pt 2:9) called to offer up the world and all that is in it—especially themselves—to the Lord of all. In exercising this office they most fully realize the meaning of our Christian stewardship. Part of what is involved here for Catholics is a stewardship of time which should include setting aside periods for family prayer, for the reading of Scripture, for visits to the blessed sacrament and for attendance at Mass during the week whenever this is possible.

Participation in Christ's redemptive activity extends even, though certainly not only, to the use people make of experiences which otherwise might seem the least promising: deprivation, loss, pain. "Now I rejoice in my sufferings for your sake," St. Paul says, "and in my flesh I am filling up what is lacking in the afflictions of Christ on behalf of his body, which is the church" (Col 1:24). Here also one looks to Jesus to lead the way. For one's estimate of suffering, as Pope John Paul points out, is transformed by discovering its "salvific meaning" when united with the suffering of Christ *(Salvifici Doloris,* 27).

Cooperation in Redemption

Penance also belongs to this aspect of Christian life. Today, as in the past, the church commends what Pope Paul VI called the "traditional triad" of prayer, fasting and almsgiving *(Paenitemini,* February 17, 1966), while also encouraging Catholics to adopt penitential practices of their own choice which suit their particular circumstances.

Through penance voluntarily accepted one gradually becomes liberated from those obstacles to Christian discipleship which a secularized culture exalting individual gratification places in one's way. These obstacles include not just the quest for pleasure but avarice, a craving for the illusion of absolute dominion and control, valuing creatures without reference to their Creator, excessive individualism and ultimately the fear of death unrelieved by hope for eternal life.

These are consequences of sin—sin which threatens the way of life of Christian stewardship and the identity of Christians as disciples of the Lord. "Let us master this great and simple truth," Cardinal Newman once said, "that all rich materials and productions of this world, being God's property, are intended for God's service; and sin only, nothing but sin, turns them to a different purpose" ("Offerings for the Sanctuary" in *Parochial and Plain Sermons* [San Francisco: Ignatius Press, 1987], p. 1368).

Sin causes people to turn in on themselves; to become grasping and exploitative toward possessions and other people; to grow accustomed to conducting relationships not by the standards of generous stewardship but by the calculus of self-interest: "What's in it for me?" Constantly Christians must beg God for the grace of conversion: the grace to know who they are, to whom they belong, how they are to live—the grace to repent and change and grow, the grace to become good disciples and stewards.

But if they do accept God's grace and, repenting, struggle to change, God will respond like the father of the prodigal son. "Filled with compassion" at seeing his repentant child approaching after a long and painful separation, this loving parent "ran to his son, embraced him and kissed him" even before the boy could stammer out the words of sorrow he had rehearsed (Lk 15:20). God's love is always there. The Spirit of wisdom and courage helps people seek pardon and be mindful, in the face of all their forgetting, that the most important work of their lives is to be Jesus' disciples.

Thus, the stewardship of disciples is not reducible only to one task or another. It involves embracing, cultivating, enjoying, sharing—and sometimes also giving up—the goods of human life. Christians live this way in the confidence which comes from faith: For they know that the human goods they cherish and cultivate will be perfected—and they themselves will be fulfilled—in that kingdom, already present, which Christ will bring to perfection and one day hand over to the Father.

IV. Stewards of the Church

When I began to provide dental treatment for persons with AIDS, I knew HIV-positive people desperately needed this service, but I did not know how much I needed them. Time and again, reaching out to serve and heal, I have found myself served and healed. Their courage, compassion, wisdom and faith have changed my life. I have faced my own mortality, and I rejoice in the daily gift of life. My love for people has taken on new dimensions. I hug and kiss my wife and family more than ever and see them as beautiful gifts from God. My ministry as a deacon has become dynamic, and I regard my profession as a vital part of it.

– Dr. Anthony M. Giambalvo,
Rockville Centre, New York

Community and Stewardship

The new covenant in and through Christ—the reconciliation he effects between humankind and God—forms a community: The new people of God, the body of Christ, the church. The unity of this people is itself a precious good, to be cherished, preserved and built up by lives of love. The Epistle to the Ephesians exhorts Christians to "live in a manner worthy of the call you have received, with all humility and gentleness, with patience, bearing with one another through love, striving to preserve the unity of the spirit through the bond of peace: one body and one Spirit, as you were also called to the one hope of your call; one Lord, one faith, one baptism; one God and Father of all" (Eph 4:1–6).

Because its individual members do collectively make up the body of Christ, that body's health and well-being are the responsibility of the members—the personal responsibility of each one of us. We all are stewards of the church. As "to each individual the manifestation of the Spirit is given for some benefit" (1 Cor 12:7), so stewardship in an ecclesial setting means cherishing and fostering the gifts of all, while using one's own gifts to serve the community of faith. The rich tradition of tithing set forth in the Old Testament is an expression of this. (See, for example, Dt 14:22, Lv 27:30.) Those who set their hearts upon spiritual gifts must "seek to have an abundance for building up the church" (1 Cor 14:12).

But how is the church built up? In a sense there are as many answers to that question as there are individual members with individual vocations.

But the overarching answer for all is this: through personal participation in and support of the church's mission of proclaiming and teaching, serving and sanctifying.

This participation takes different forms according to people's different gifts and offices, but there is a fundamental obligation arising from the sacrament of baptism (cf. Pope John Paul II, *Christifideles Laici,* 15): that people place their gifts, their resources—themselves—at God's service in and through the church. Here also Jesus is the model. Even though his perfect self-emptying is unique, it is within the power of disciples, and a duty, that they be generous stewards of the church, giving freely of their time, talent and treasure. "Consider this," Paul says, addressing not only the Christians of Corinth but all of us. "Whoever sows sparingly will also reap sparingly, and whoever sows bountifully will also reap bountifully....God loves a cheerful giver" (2 Cor 9:6–7).

Evangelization and Stewardship

In various ways, then, stewardship of the church leads people to share in the work of evangelization or proclaiming the good news, in the work of catechesis or transmitting and strengthening the faith, and in works of justice and mercy on behalf of persons in need. Stewardship requires support for the church's institutions and programs for these purposes. But according to their opportunities and circumstances, members of the church also should engage in such activities personally and on their own initiative.

Parents, for instance, have work of great importance to do in the domestic church, the home. Within the family they must teach their children the truths of the faith and pray with them, share Christian values with them in the face of pressures to conform to the hostile values of a secularized society and initiate them into the practice of stewardship itself, in all its dimensions, contrary to today's widespread consumerism and individualism. This may require adjusting the family's own patterns of consumption and its lifestyle, including the use of television and other media which sometimes preach values in conflict with the mind of Christ. Above all it requires that parents themselves be models of stewardship, especially by their selfless service to one another, to their children and to church and community needs.

Parishes, too, must be, or become, true communities of faith within which this Christian way of life is learned and practiced. Sound business practice is a fundamental of good stewardship, and stewardship as it relates to church finances must include the most stringent ethical, legal and fiscal standards. That requires several things: Pastors and parish staff must be open, consultative, collegial and accountable in the conduct of affairs. And parishioners must accept responsibility for their parishes and contribute generously—both money and personal service—to their programs and projects. The success or failure of parish programs, the vitality of parish life or its absence, the ability or inability of a parish to render needed services to its members and the community depends upon all.

We, therefore, urge the Catholics of every parish in our land to ponder the words of St. Paul: "Now as you excel in every respect, in faith, discourse, knowledge, all earnestness, and in the love we have for you, may you excel in this gracious act also" (2 Cor 8:7). Only by living as generous stewards of these local Christian communities, their parishes, can the Catholics of the United States hope to make them the vital sources of faith-filled Christian dynamism they are meant to be.

At the same time, stewardship in and for the parish should not be narrowly parochial. For the diocese is not merely an administrative structure but instead joins communities called parishes into a "local church" and unites its people in faith, worship and service. The same spirit of personal responsibility in which a Catholic approaches his or her parish should extend to the diocese and be expressed in essentially the same ways: generous material support and self-giving. As in the case of the parish, too, lay Catholics ought to have an active role in the oversight of the stewardship of pastoral leaders and administrators at the diocesan level. At the present time it seems clear that many Catholics need to develop a better understanding of the financial needs of the church at the diocesan level. Indeed, the spirit and practice of stewardship should extend to other local churches and to the universal church—to the Christian community and to one's sisters and brothers in Christ everywhere—and be expressed in deeds of service and mutual support. For some this will mean direct personal participation in evangelization and mission work, for others generous giving to the collections established for these purposes and other worthy programs.

Every member of the church is called to evangelize, and the practice of authentic Christian stewardship inevitably leads to evangelization. As stewards of the mysteries of God (1 Cor 4:1), people desire to tell others about them and about the light they shed on human life, to share the gifts and graces they have received from God, especially knowledge of Christ Jesus, "who became for us wisdom from God, as well as righteousness, sanctification and redemption" (1 Cor 1:30). Human beings, says Pope Paul VI, "have the right to know the riches of the mystery of Christ. It is in these...that the whole human family can find in the most comprehensive form and beyond all their expectations everything for which they have been groping" *(Evangelii Nuntiandi,* 53).

Solidarity and Stewardship

While the unity arising from the covenant assumes and requires human solidarity, it also goes beyond it, producing spiritual fruit insofar as it is founded on union with the Lord. "I am the vine, you are the branches," Jesus says. "Whoever remains in me and I in him will bear much fruit" (Jn 15:5). As Simone Weil remarks, "A single piece of bread given to a hungry man is enough to save a soul—if it is given in the right way.

In this world, however, solidarity encounters many obstacles on both the individual and social levels. It is essential that Jesus' disciples do what can be done to remove them.

The most basic and pervasive obstacle is sheer selfish lack of love, a lack which people must acknowledge and seek to correct when they find it in their own hearts and lives. For the absence of charity from the lives of disciples of Jesus in itself is self-defeating and hypocritical. "If anyone says, 'I love God,' but hates his brother, he is a liar" (1 Jn 4:20).

Extreme disparities in wealth and power also block unity and communion. Such disparities exist today between person and person, social class and social class, nation and nation. They are contrary to that virtue of solidarity, grounded in charity, which Pope John Paul commends as the basis of a world order embodying "a new model of the unity of the human race" whose "supreme model" is the intimate life of the Trinity itself *(Sollicitudo Rei Socialis,* 40). Familiarity with the church's growing body of social doctrine is necessary in order to grasp and respond to the practical requirements of discipleship and stewardship in light of the complex realities of today's national and international socioeconomic life.

Social justice, which the pastoral letter "Economic Justice for All" calls a kind of contributive justice, is a particular aspect of the virtue of solidarity. Encompassing the duty of "all who are able to create the goods, services and other non-material or spiritual values necessary for the welfare of the whole community," it gives moral as well as economic content to the concept of productivity. Thus productivity "cannot be measured solely by its output of goods and services." Rather, "patterns of productivity must...measured in light of their impact on the fulfillment of basic needs, employment levels, patterns of discrimination, environmental impact and sense of community" ("Economic Justice for All," 72).

Finally, and most poignantly, solidarity is obstructed by the persistence of religious conflicts and divisions, including those which sunder even followers of Christ. Christians remain tragically far from realizing Jesus' priestly prayer "that they may all be one, as you, Father, are in me and I in you" (Jn 17:21).

As all this suggests, our individual lives as disciples and stewards must be seen in relation to God's larger purposes. From the outset of his covenanting, God had it in mind to make many one. He promised Abram: "I will make of you a great nation, and I will bless you; I will make your name great, so that you will be a blessing....All the communities of the earth shall find blessing in you" (Gen 12:2–3). In Jesus, the kingdom of God is inaugurated—a kingdom open to all. Those who enter into Jesus' new covenant find themselves growing in a union of minds and hearts with others who also have responded to God's call. They find their hearts and minds expanding to embrace all men and women, especially those in need, in a communion of mercy and love.

Eucharistic Stewardship

The eucharist is the great sign and agent of this expansive communion of charity. "Because the loaf of bread is one, we, though many, are one body, for we all partake of the one loaf" (1 Cor 10:17). Here people enjoy a unique union with Christ and, in him, with one another. Here his love—indeed, his very self—flows into his disciples and, through them and their practice of stewardship, to the entire human race. Here Jesus renews his covenant-forming act of perfect fidelity to God, while also making it possible for us to cooperate. In the eucharist Christians reaffirm their participation in the new covenant, they give thanks to God for blessings received and they strengthen their bonds of commitment to one another as members of the covenant community Jesus forms.

And what do Christians bring to the eucharistic celebration and join there with Jesus' offering? Their lives as Christian disciples: their personal vocations and the stewardship they have exercised regarding them, their individual contributions to the great work of restoring all things in Christ. Disciples give thanks to God for gifts received and strive to share them with others. That is why, as Vatican II says of the eucharist, "if this celebration is to be sincere and thorough, it must lead to various works of charity and mutual help, as well as to missionary activity and to different forms of Christian witness" *(Presbyterorum Ordinis,* 6).

More than that, the eucharist is the sign and agent of that heavenly communion in which we shall together share, enjoying the fruits of stewardship "freed of stain, burnished and transfigured" *(Gaudium et Spes,* 39). It is not only the promise but the commencement of the heavenly banquet where human lives are perfectly fulfilled.

We have Jesus' word for it: "Whoever eats this bread will live forever; and the bread that I will give is my flesh for the life of the world" (Jn 6:51). The glory and the boast of Christian stewards lie in mirroring, however poorly, the stewardship of Jesus Christ, who gave and still gives all he has and is, in order to be faithful to God's will and carry through to completion his redemptive stewardship of human beings and their world.

V. The Christian Steward

> It was 16 years ago, but it seems like only yesterday. I was suddenly confronted with serious surgery, which I never thought would happen to me. It always happened to others. The memory is still there and I recall vividly the days before the surgery. I really received the grace to ask myself, "What do I own, and what owns me?"
>
> When you are wheeled into a surgery room, it really doesn't matter who you are or what you possess. What counts is the confidence in a competent surgical staff and a good and gracious God.
>
> I know that my whole understanding and appreciation of the gifts and resources I possess took on new meaning. It is amazing how a divine economy of life and health provide a unique perspective of what really matters.
>
> – Archbishop Thomas Murphy of Seattle

While the New Testament does not provide a rounded portrait of the Christian steward all in one place, elements of such a portrait are present throughout its pages.

In the Gospel, Jesus speaks of the "faithful and prudent steward" as one whom a householder sets over other members of the household in order to "distribute the food allowance at the proper time" (Lk 12:42; cf. Mt 24:25). Evidently, good stewards understand that they are to share with others what they have received, that this must be done in a timely way and that God will hold them accountable for how well or badly they do it. For if a steward wastes the owner's goods and mistreats the other household members, "that servant's master will come on an unexpected day and at an unknown hour and will punish him severely and assign him a place with the unfaithful" (Lk 12:46).

In the lives of disciples, however, something else must come before the practice of stewardship. They need a flash of insight—a certain way of seeing—by which they view the world and their relationship to it in a fresh, new light. "The world is charged with the grandeur of God," Gerard Manley Hopkins exclaims. More than anything else, it may be this glimpse of the divine grandeur in all that is which sets people on the path of Christian stewardship.

Not only in material creation do people discern God present and active, but also, and especially, in the human heart.

"Do not be deceived....All good giving and every perfect gift is from above" (Jas 1:17), and this is true above all where spiritual gifts are concerned. Various as they are, "one and the same Spirit produces all of these" (1 Cor 12:11)—including the gift of discernment itself, which leads men and women to say: "We have not received the spirit of the world but the Spirit that is from God, so that we may understand the things freely given us by God" (1 Cor 2:12). So it is that people have the power to live as stewards, striving to realize the ideal set forth by Paul: "Whether you eat or drink, or whatever you do, do everything for the glory of God" (1 Cor 10:31).

Christian stewards are conscientious and faithful. After all, the first requirement of a steward is to be "found trustworthy" (1 Cor 4:2). In the present case, moreover, stewardship is a uniquely solemn trust. If Christians understand it and strive to live it to the full, they grasp the fact that they are no less than "God's co-workers" (1 Cor 3:9), with their own particular share in his creative, redemptive and sanctifying work. In this light, stewards are fully conscious of their accountability. They neither live nor die as their own masters; rather, "if we live, we live for the Lord, and if we die, we die for the Lord; so then, whether we live or die, we are the Lord's" (Rom 14:8).

Christian stewards are generous out of love as well as duty. They dare not fail in charity and what it entails, and the New Testament is filled with warnings to those who might be tempted to substitute some counterfeit for authentic love. For example: "If someone who has worldly means sees a brother in need and refuses him compassion, how can the love of God remain in him?" (1 Jn 3:17). Or this: "Come now, you rich, weep and wail over your impending miseries. Your wealth has rotted away, your clothes have become moth-eaten, your gold and silver have corroded and that corrosion will be a testimony against you; it will devour your flesh like a fire. You have stored up treasure for the last days" (Jas 5:1–3).

What, then, are Christians to do? Of course people's lives as stewards take countless forms, according to their unique vocations and circumstances. Still, the fundamental pattern in every case is simple and changeless: "Serve one another through love....Bear one another's burdens, and so you will fulfill the law of Christ" (Gal 5:13, 6:2). This includes being stewards of the church, for, as we are quite specifically told, "the church of the living God" is "the household of God" (1 Tm 3:15), and it is essential to practice stewardship there.

The life of a Christian steward, lived in imitation of the life of Christ, is challenging, even difficult in many ways; but both here and hereafter it is charged with intense joy. Like Paul, the good steward is able to say, "I am filled with encouragement, I am overflowing with joy all the more because of all our affliction" (2 Cor 7:4). Women and men who seek to live in this way learn that "all things work for good for those who love God" (Rom 8:28). It is part of their personal experience that God is "rich in mercy (and) we are his handiwork, created in Christ Jesus for the good works that God has prepared in advance, that we should live in them" (Eph 2:4, 10). They readily cry out from the heart: "Rejoice in the Lord always! I shall say it again: Rejoice!" (Phil 4:4).

They look forward in hope to hearing the Master's words addressed to those who have lived as disciples faithful in their practice of stewardship should: "Come, you who are blessed by my Father. Inherit the kingdom prepared for you from the foundation of the world" (Mt 25:34).

After Jesus, it is the Blessed Virgin Mary who by her example most perfectly teaches the meaning of discipleship and stewardship in their fullest sense. All of their essential elements are found in her life: She was called and gifted by God, she responded generously, creatively and prudently, she understood her divinely assigned role as "handmaid" in terms of service and fidelity (Lk 1:26–56).

As mother of God, her stewardship consisted of her maternal service and devotion to Jesus, from infancy to adulthood, up to the agonizing hours of Jesus' death (Jn 19:25). As mother of the church, her stewardship is clearly articulated in the closing chapter of the Second Vatican Council's Constitution on the Church, *Lumen Gentium* (cf. 52–69). Pope John Paul observes: "Mary is one of the first who 'believed,' and precisely with her faith as spouse and mother she wishes to act upon all those who entrust themselves to her as children" *(Redemptoris Mater,* 46).

In light of all this, it only remains for all of us to ask ourselves this question: Do we also wish to be disciples of Jesus Christ? The Spirit is ready to show us the way—a way of which stewardship is a part.

Genesis, telling the story of creation, says God looked upon what had been made and found it good; and seeing the world's goodness, God entrusted it to human beings. "The Lord God planted a garden" and placed there human persons "to cultivate and care for it" (Gen 2:8, 15). Now, as then and always, it is a central part of the human vocation that we be good stewards of what we have received—this garden, this divine-human workshop, this world and all that is in it—setting minds and hearts and hands to the task of creating and redeeming in cooperation with our God, creator and Lord of all.

(*Origins*, December 17, 1992, Vol. 22: No. 27)

Bibliography

The Internet is a significant research tool and should be used in conjunction with any of the following.

Albrecht, Karl and Ron Zemke. *Service America: Doing Business in the New Economy*. Homewood, Ill.: Dow Jones-Irwin, 1985.

Black, Henry Campbell. *Black's Law Dictionary*, 7th edition. St. Paul, Minn.: West Publishing Co., 1999.

Brakeley, George A. *Tested Ways to Successful Fund Raising*. New York: Amacom, 1980.

Clements, C. Justin. *The Steward's Way*. Kansas City, Mo.: Sheed & Ward, 1997.

Coriden, James A. *The Parish in Catholic Tradition: History, Theology, and Canon Law*. Mahwah, N.J.: Paulist Press, 1997.

Edles, L. Peter. *Fundraising: Hands-On Tactics for Nonprofit Groups*. New York: McGraw-Hill, 1993.

Flanagan, Joan. *Successful Fundraising*. Chicago: Contemporary Books, 1993.

Flanagan, Joan. *The Grass Roots Fundraising Book: How to Raise Money in Your Community*. Chicago: Contemporary Books, 1995.

Gaby, Patricia V. *Nonprofit Organization Handbook: A Guide to Fund Raising, Grants, Lobbying, Membership Building, Publicity, and Public Relations*. Englewood Cliffs, N.J.: Prentice-Hall, 1979.

Gilpatrick, Eleanor. *Grants for Nonprofit Organizations*. Westport, Conn.: Praeger Publications, 1989.

Greeley, Andrew, and William McManus. *Catholic Contributions: Sociology and Public Policy.* Chicago: The Thomas More Press, 1987.

Greenfield, James M. *Fund-Raising Fundamentals.* New York: John Wiley & Sons, Inc., 1994.

Hoge, Dean R. *Money Matters: Personal Giving in American Churches.* Louisville, Ken.: Westminster John Knox Press, 1996.

Hueckel, Sharon. *Stewardship by the Book.* Kansas City, Mo.: Sheed & Ward, 1996.

Huels, John M., O.S.M., J.C.D. *The Pastoral Companion—A Canon Law Handbook for Catholic Ministry.* Chicago: The Franciscan Herald Press, 1986.

Jarboe, John B. "Undue Influence & Gifts to Religious Organizations." *Catholic Lawyer,* Vol. 35, No.3, pp. 271–282.

Keegan, P. Burke. *Fundraising for Non-Profits.* New York: Harper Perennial, 1990.

Lant, J. *Development Today—A Fund-Raising Guide for Non-Profit Organizations.* Cambridge, Mass.: JLA Publications, 1990.

Margolin, Judith. *The Individual's Guide to Grants.* New York: Plenum Press, 1983.

McNamara, Patrick, and Charles Zech. "Lagging Stewards." *America,* September 14, 1996, Vol. 175, No.6., pp. 9–14.

National Catholic Stewardship Council, Inc. *Stewardship—Disciples Respond: A Practical Guide for Pastoral Leaders.* Washington, D.C., 1997.

National Conference of Catholic Bishops, Ad Hoc Committee on Stewardship. *Stewardship and Development in Catholic Dioceses and Parishes Resource Manual.* Washington, D.C., 1996.

National Conference of Catholic Bishops/United States Catholic Conference. *Stewardship: A Disciple's Response.* Washington, D.C., 1993.

New, Anne L. *Raise More Money for Your Nonprofit Organization.* New York: The Foundation Center, 1991.

Ray, George McNeill. *Tall in His Presence.* Greenwich, Conn.: Seabury Press, 1961.

Ronsvalle, John & Sylvia. *Behind the Stained Glass Windows.* Grand Rapids, Mich.: Baker Books, 1996.

Rosso, Henry A. and Associates. *Achieving Excellence in Fund Raising.* San Francisco: Jossey-Bass, 1991.

St. Francis of Assisi Parish. *Stewardship: Living Life As God Intended: A Program for Your Parish.* Wichita, Kan.

Scheets, O.S.C., Francis Kelly, and Joseph Claude Harris. "Is the Sunday Collection in Trouble?" *America*, July 15, 1995, Vol. 173, No. 2, pp. 18–20.

Swartz, Rita McCarthy. *How to Present a Ministry Fair*. Kansas City, Mo.: Sheed & Ward, 1996.

Taylor, Bernard P. "Guide to Successful Fund-Raising for Authentic Charitable Purposes"; Groupwork Today, South Plainfield, N.J.: 1976.

Thompson, Thomas K. *Stewardship in Contemporary Theology*. New York: Association Press, 1960.

Warner, Irving R. *The Art of Fund-Raising*. Rockville, Md.: Fund-Raising Institute, 1992.

Zech, Charles E. *Why Catholics Don't Give…And What Can Be Done About It*. Huntington, Ind.: Our Sunday Visitor, 2000.

Index